KEEP CLIMBING

KEEP

ATRIA BOOKS

CLIMBING

SEAN SWARNER

With Rusty Fischer

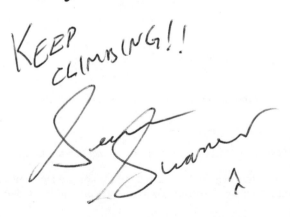

KEEP CLIMBING!!

NEW YORK · LONDON · TORONTO · SYDNEY

ATRIA BOOKS
1230 Avenue of the Americas
New York, NY 10020

Library of Congress Cataloging-in-Publication Data

Swarner, Sean.
Keep climbing / Sean Swarner.
p.   cm.
1. Swarner, Sean—Health.   2. Hodgkin's disease—Patients—Biography.
3. Cancer—Patients—Biography.   I. Title.

RC644.S95   2007
362.196'994460092—dc22
[B]   2006047939

ISBN-13: 978-0-7432-9205-4
ISBN-10: 0-7432-9205-7

First Atria Books hardcover edition February 2007

1   3   5   7   9   10   8   6   4   2

ATRIA BOOKS is a trademark of Simon & Schuster, Inc.

Photo Credits: Unless otherwise credited, all photos are from the author's
collection. Insert: p. 1 bottom, courtesy of *Mansfield News Journal*.

Manufactured in the United States of America

For information about special discounts for bulk purchases,
please contact Simon & Schuster Special Sales at
1-800-456-6798 or business@simonandschuster.com.

Dedicated to all those affected by cancer in this small world.

Keep Climbing!

CONTENTS

❖

KEEP CLIMBING

VIEW FROM THE TOP

❖

The silk-screened flag flaps in the stiff breeze at the top of the world. I can already tell that by week's end, its edges will be tattered from the constant battering, looking worse for the wear but still mostly intact. In a few weeks it will be skeletal, a mere shadow of itself; in months it will be little more than a stick in the snow and some frayed fabric.

But that's okay.

This close to heaven, what are a few loose ends, right?

The funny thing is, even with all these months of preparation, training, and planning, I'd naively assumed mine would be the only flag up here. It's not; the top of Everest is like one of those roadside shrines you see everywhere these days, where someone has died in a horrible accident. Only, instead of teddy bears and plastic daisies, you see prayer flags, pickets, and Perlon stacked in an unceremonial, if colorful, heap on the snowy, narrow summit.

I ignore the tackiness, the gaudiness, and admire the flag anyway. People climb Everest for dozens of reasons, but for me this is more than some mere personal odyssey. The flag, tattered though it soon may be, represents the hopes, the dreams, and in some cases the dying wishes of countless people diagnosed with cancer.

I know I'm one of the incredibly lucky ones.

It's 9:32 A.M. on the sixteenth of May, 2002, and I'm standing at the highest point on the planet. The summit of Everest: 29,035 feet. Below me is the globe, that thing you spin in elementary school, never looking past the big red star that marks the capital of your home state.

That's the view from the top.

You can actually see the curvature of the earth. That's right. (If Magellan had just been a mountaineer, he would have saved himself a lot of sailing.) It's really round. In the distance you can see the planet slope, curving gently amid the craggy outcroppings of mountainous terrain that are the Himalayas; stand here long enough, and I swear it would feel like a carnival ride.

Here, too, at approximately the altitude where jumbo jets level off and soar through the atmosphere, the stars are at eye level. Amazing. Truly. If it were a few hours earlier and I had a lasso, the moon would be, well, you know the rest.

You would think there'd be some privacy at the top of the world, but it's smaller than you imagine, and crowded. Picture the highest putt-putt course in the galaxy: You've got climbers turning around for the trek down, those who have just summitted and are still giddy with a sense of accomplishment, and those you passed along the way, trudging inexorably forward, nipping at your heels. And in this ultimate game of King of the Mountain, they all want to knock you off.

I smile at the irony, but it was one of many I'd enjoyed during the last two months I'd spent in Nepal. Who'd have guessed that only a few days earlier, at Camp 3, I'd spoken by two-way radio to a doctor from Brown University who had strongly suggested that I take the infamous line test to check for altitude-induced cerebral edema.

The line test is like a field sobriety test, where you put one foot in front of the other in a straight line. Heel, toe, heel, toe. Right, left, right, left. Not too tough, right? Well, at 24,000 feet on the side of the Lhotse Face, it's difficult to find a foot of flat surface to try to do this test, let alone enough elbow room to walk it off. Somehow I found about three feet of flat surface to try walking the line.

After taking about thirty minutes to put on my boots, I was back outside my tent, feeling deflated. I was sucking O's (Everest-speak for oxygen) and wasn't feeling well at all. I tried the line test and called my brother, Seth, on the radio.

He radioed back to me: "So, how'd it go?"

My silence must have been deafening. When he repeated "Hello?," he sounded about like I felt.

"Yeah, I'm here," I finally responded.

"So, how'd it go?"

The line test is one that pretty much sums up your mental capabilities and your physical ability to perform at altitude. It could also detect the beginning stages of HACE (high-altitude cerebral edema). *Major* problem!

"Sean, do you copy?"

"Yes, I copy."

"How'd the test go?"

"You want the truth?" By now tears were flowing down my cheeks. I couldn't put one foot in front of the other without looking or acting like a complete drunk. I could focus, but I couldn't do the test to save my life.

"I couldn't do it, Seth. At all." More silence. "Now what?"

After some discussion, we decided I should stay on O's and take a Diamox (high-altitude medicine). Not something I really like doing, since I've had enough drugs pumped into my body from the chemo and all that other good stuff over the years to qualify me as a walking toxic dump.

So I stayed at Camp 3, sucking O's and trying to feel better. I slept at Camp 3 yet another night as well. During both the day and night, I focused on feeling better and not letting any negative thoughts into my head. It's amazing how mental being physical can be, but at this stage of the game, your heart isn't only a muscle, it's also equal parts troop leader, physical trainer, and drill sergeant. Heading out of Camp 3, I was jamming along to my MP3 player, streaming tunes and keeping my head focused on the task at hand.

The rest came in handy: The summit push that morning had been as brutal and unrelenting as I'd expected, and it had lasted twice as long. My age and fitness level were in the plus column; my past history with chemo and chemical cocktails, combined with a compromised immune system and a damaged lung from the radiation therapy, definitely weighed down the minus column.

I'd come this far. There was no way I was backing down now.

The famed and notorious Hillary Step halfway between the South Summit and the main summit, at 28,800 feet, was to be my biggest hurdle. I don't mind telling you old Sir Edmund had me by the short hairs as I stood at its base.

When I looked up at the sheer ascent, massive gray slate bordered by slick, treacherous ice, I might as well have been staring at the sheer face of some mirrored building in downtown L.A. It rose straight up and looked nasty; everything I'd heard, all the warnings, the doom and gloom—for once, they were right.

On the websites, the digicams, the photos posted far and wide in e-mails and on blog boards, Everest looks like a gently sloping giant, a pyramid with plenty of footbridges and handholds (I call that the "Vegas version").

Up close and personal, it's quite a different story. Here, wind gusts reach well over a hundred miles an hour for minutes at a time—and often at the most *inopportune* moment—and then suddenly stop, leaving you breathless and quaking in their wake, scrambling for purchase and moving double time, eager to get as far and as high as possible before the wind gusts again.

Here, too, the fear of dreaded HACE is a constant threat. This is when the brain swells and ceases to function properly. HACE can progress rapidly and be fatal in a matter of a few hours to one or two days. People with this illness are often confused and may not recognize that they are ill. Eventually, they would experience a loss of consciousness and, ultimately, death. Divers who plumb the planet's depths get the bends when they've gone too deep for too long and try to rise too fast. High-altitude climbers get HACE.

Above it all I strode, footstep after footstep, ever upward, ever onward, guided by my fearless Sherpas, Nima Gombu, and Kame, and their pleasant, broad, smiling faces, uttering words of encouragement even as I struggled up the treacherous Hillary Step, my breathing ragged, my lungs begging for more air.

This from a kid who, despite several months of intense training for this very trek, had been only as high as 14,600 feet.

At 9:32 A.M. on the sixteenth of May, I made my way up the Hillary Step and onto the summit of the highest peak in the world. I immediately radioed down to Base Camp and asked for my brother.

Immediately, Seth was on the radio. Here is our actual transmission from that day:

"Hello?"

"Seth?"

"Yeah."

"You can let everyone know that Seth Swarner's brother made it to the top of the world!"

"You made it?"

"Yeah, I'm on Everest."

"I'm crying like a little baby."

"Me, too."

After a while the connection was severed, and I was alone—or at least alone as possible—at the highest peak of my own physical and personal summit. I stood, with my windburned face, chapped lips, eyes shielded by the latest glacier sunglasses, bright orange snow gear, signaling to the world that a kid who'd been told twice in one lifetime he had two weeks to live now had the accomplishment of a lifetime under his belt.

I suppose I shouldn't have been so surprised. Cancer hadn't beaten me.

Why should the world's tallest mountain?

The silk-screened flag flaps in the stiff breeze at the top of the world. Its sound is subtle, instantly recognizable, and reassuring. It brags, "You made it, Sean. You did it. You've made history. First and only cancer survivor to climb the world's tallest mountain."

Then it whispers, "And we climbed it with you. All of us. Every name on this flag, every person ever affected by cancer in any way; we're here with you, here for you, right now and always."

Then another eighty-mile-an-hour gust at the top of the world scatters the whispers to all four corners of the globe. I look around to see if anybody else hears it. Nothing.

It's just me and the flag and the highest point on the planet. I watch the Sherpas mill around, I suck in a little O_2 to get ready for the more dangerous climb down, and I use most of it reading off the names listed on the flag:

"Suzanne Miller.

"Dante Richards.

"Oscar Jones.

"Dennis Maltz.

"Alicia Watts . . ."

It sucks me dry, but I read them all, one by one. Even those names my brother and I handwrote and added at the last second before I started my ascent. I take a picture, knowing I'm going to send a copy to everyone on the flag, with inspirational words of encouragement written on the back of each one. The Sherpas look impatient, the fabric of their snowsuits rustling as they pace at nearly 30,000 feet, eager to get me back down the mountain safely.

I sigh, finish the list, and look over the edge of the world while tears run down my face.

A line is forming. Can you believe it? Here, of all places, stands a queue of brightly colored snowsuits looking like Skittles in the blinding white snow right after the awe-inspiring South Summit and before the Hillary Step. They're all waiting for their shot, their own personal listing in the record books of their own lives.

I've overextended my stay. I look back at the flag, bearing the names of all those affected by cancer, dozens of them, hundreds, names stacked one on top of the other like the climbers in their queue. The breeze picks up and the flag flaps; already it's bending to the blur of the elements, its edges starting to tatter its ink starting to fade.

But that's okay.

This close to heaven, what are a few loose ends, right?

CHAPTER ONE

ADOLESCENCE, INTERRUPTED

❖

I suppose I've always been a climber. From trees to hills to arbors to piles of debris, if there was something higher than ground level and I was awake, you could pretty much find me on top of it.

Walking down the baby-blue hallway that late January day in 1988, I turned left and entered the Willard Junior High School gymnasium on the balls of my feet and without a care in the world.

There was a stage with a small workout room to the right, and the pegboards I usually climbed directly in front of me on the left wall. Typically, I would already be scrambling up there, the pegs solid and comforting in my hands as I reached ever higher, scaling up to the ceiling and back a few times before a friend or two told me it was time to get to our next class.

For some reason, we weren't allowed to climb the pegboard that day. Who knows why? Perhaps it was closed for repairs, or maybe the teacher watching the gym that day didn't want to get the pegs for us. Either way, it looked like my climbing fix would have to wait until the next day.

Instead, I picked up a game of basketball with some other friends. My new Nike high-tops squeaked across the varnished gym floor as I drove for the basket. Squeak. Turn. Squeak. Pivot.

Squeak-squeak. It was music to my ears, and much more than the mere sound of rubber on hardwood floor; it was the sound of basketball itself.

Sweat, clean and clear, dripped off my nose as my chest burned from lugging the ball up one end of the court and back down the other. We'd been taking our time, hotdogging it for the smattering of Madonna wannabes lined up against the gym wall, but now it was put-up-or-shut-up time.

"Come on, Sean," shouted a red-faced opponent, pissed because his team was down by six points, "lunch period's almost over. Shoot already!"

I smiled, gave him the finger with my free hand, and drove the ball with my other. It smacked against the floor, solid and right, traveling back to my long fingers as if magnetized. It followed me where I went, left, right, defying the laws of gravity and physics, always finding my hand no matter how far I'd run up-court.

I shucked, I jived, I zigged, I zagged until at last the basket was in plain sight. I flew through their defenders, a lackluster group of pudgy kids playing hooky from shop class, and stole toward the basket with my buddies playing defense the whole way there.

There was Jerry, my neighbor and longtime sleepover pal, whose dad had the best dirty-magazine collection this side of the Cuyahoga River. There was Scott, who always had a stick of gum in his mouth and a smartass answer for the teacher. How could I forget Andy, who had the hottest sister in town and never let me forget it, either.

Jerking forward with the ball, I was closing in for an easy layup and a quick two points for our team. The squeaking followed me, an angry half-dozen defenders all trying to catch up, but I was too fast for them. I'd always been too fast. Just as my feet left the ground, a grossly audible snap came from my left knee.

I heard it before I felt it, and neither the sound nor the sensation was pleasant. Think King Arthur ripping off a turkey leg in every old Knights of the Round Table movie you've ever seen, gristle tearing and flesh loosing and the empty, hollow thwock of joint leaving joint: That was the sound and the sensation. I tumbled to the hardwood floor with a thump, holding my leg, rolling around on the ground in pain as the game came to an abrupt halt.

My bare elbows and shins sang out in pain as they smacked against the hardwood floor, me writhing to and fro as I reached for my offended knee, flinging sweat from my hair as I shook my head, pain and frustration contorting my features into an unrecognizable mask.

This can't be happening, I remember thinking. *I had two easy points, right there on the board. We could have shut them out!*

Then all was dark. There are a few lost minutes in my memory—either I passed out or freaked out or both. The next thing I remember is my buddies picking me up. The looks on their faces said it all: This was bad. The game was over, the grimy shop kids trading high fives and smug glances as they watched me hobble to my feet.

I didn't want to give them the satisfaction. I tried to brush off the injury and keep playing, but the pain forced me to totter over to the stage and sit out for the rest of the period before hobbling to my science class, an athlete in his prime benched over by the Bunsen burners, taking notes instead of signing autographs.

After struggling through the rest of the day, limping from class to class, I was relieved to hear the bell signaling the day was finally over. Next came the long trek home. I sighed and gathered the books from my locker that I'd need for homework that night. Then I tucked them under my arm and started off for home.

I don't remember much of that walk from school, except trying to talk myself out of the pain. *It's nothing,* I remember telling myself, limping along like Frankenstein, dragging my left leg to keep up with my right. *Walk it off, Sean. Isn't that what Coach would say? Walk it off.*

I walked it off, all right, but it wasn't easy. By the time I got home, my knee had swollen to roughly the size of a grapefruit and looked horribly discolored, as if someone had taken aim and splattered it with black, yellow, and blue paintballs. Think bruise, then think bruise in 3-D Technicolor. Then plug it in. That was my knee. My mom took one look at it and called the local doctor.

It was a simple thing, really, something any mom would do for her son. But that call signaled the beginning of the end of life as I knew it. By picking up the phone and dialing those seven simple digits, my mom had effectively sentenced me to several years of pain, fear, depression, rage, self-pity, and, finally, triumph.

Then again, if she hadn't made the call, the sentence would have been far worse.

In the span of one pickup-basketball game, I had gone from a typical middle school student to a walking—make that a limping—science experiment. Nobody knew what was wrong with me. Not Dr. Rosso, the family physician my mom called that day, a tidy middle-aged man who was used to treating sore throats and tummyaches and not fruit-sized limbs. Not the knee specialist in Mansfield, Ohio, to whom he referred us.

I spent the rest of that afternoon alternating between waiting rooms and doctors' offices, reading months-old *Highlights* magazines, favoring my right leg and answering a lot of questions that didn't add up to much. The knee specialist couldn't do an X-ray because my swollen knee wouldn't fit in his machine, and all I got from the glorified immobilizer cast he gave me was a lot of attention from my mom, dad, and younger brother, Seth.

The rest of that afternoon and evening, I could barely keep my eyes open at the dinner table, and that was after taking a nap. Right after dinner, it was straight to bed, and that was the first night I ever understood what people meant when they said they were asleep before their head hit the pillow.

The next thing I knew, my mom was shaking me awake, and sun was streaming through my bedroom window. She said that I had slept through my alarm clock—another first—but that was one of many I was in store for on that grim day of days.

Suddenly, my mom called my dad into the room. By the time I fully woke up, they were both hovering above me, staring down with eyes wide open and mouths agape, as if I'd been disfigured in a horrible car accident.

I might as well have been: Every single joint in my body had swollen to the point that my mom and dad later told me they thought they were looking at the Pillsbury Doughboy. I was all flesh and fluid, ringlets of bright pink skin swollen to bursting at my elbows, knees, wrists, ankles, you name it; if two bones met, my young, elastic skin was shiny and swollen.

They didn't even recognize their own son lying in his bed.

Bed. That was where I'd be spending much of the next four days, at the local hospital, surrounded by doctors and nurses, all of them wanting something from me: blood, urine, stool samples, my temperature, more blood, more samples. A throat culture here, a swab there, a pinprick here, a tube there. On and on and on it went, time passing in increments of plastic trays and empty vials, cute nurses and those not so cute.

There was no time to enjoy missing school, no time to thank the visitors who paraded in and out, no time to answer the get-well cards and bouquets of flowers that stood sentinel over me that week. There was only the fear of the unknown: What did I have, and how was I going to get rid of it?

After I'd spent four days lying on my back in that hospital bed, being poked, prodded, and tested, the doctor came to talk to my family. Dr. Rosso, who'd originally suggested I see a knee special-ist and now realized that the knee was the least of my worries, pulled my mom and dad out into the hallway to ask them a ques-tion.

A question that, once they shared it with me, would resonate with me for the rest of my life: "Teri, Scott," he said hesitantly, a sigh escaping his thin, dry lips, "do you know of any good oncol-ogists?"

At the time I had no idea what an oncologist was, but rest as-sured, my mom and dad sure did. They broke down and started crying, and that was when I knew something wasn't right. This wasn't pneumonia or the measles or anything else I could put a name to. Mom and Dad went for a walk down the hallway to gather themselves before coming back into my room.

I watched them come at me, their shoes squeaking on the heavily varnished hospital floors. It seemed to take them forever, as if they were dragging their feet. Squeak. Drag.

Squeak.

Drag.

I sighed, closed my eyes, and rested them against my soft white hospital pillow. Squeak. Drag. Squeak. I remembered the squeak of my new shoes against the basketball court only days—God, had it only been days?—earlier. The dripping sweat, the thumping heart, the pounding adrenaline, and the pull of my knee away from the rest of me.

I smiled, then grimaced, blushing at the bittersweet memory. I must have dozed off, the quiet beep of the machines in my room lulling me. I woke to find my parents at my bedside, looking frail and empty. I knew they were there to comfort me, but it looked like they were the ones who needed the comforting.

I tried to remember what had happened just before I fell asleep. Dr. Rosso talking, Mom and Dad hovering, conferring in the hall, crying in each other's arms, and that word, what was it again?

Oncologist. That was it. But what did it mean? I wanted to know how a simple word, spoken by our family doctor, could have such a strange effect on my parents. I asked them to tell me. They did. They had to. They were my parents; they alone couldn't lie to me.

I watched in quiet anticipation as they stumbled over the words, leaning on each other for support, trying to be strong, and all I heard was the shuffling of their nervous feet on the linoleum floor of my hospital. Shuffle. Squeak. Shuffle.

It's funny how easily—and quickly—your life can be separated into before and after. I'd had my before. The lunch bell five days earlier. Standing in line. Joking with my friends. Hassling the lunch ladies with the rest of the guys. Apologizing with my eyes when they weren't looking. Fishing out my $1.50 for lunch. Beefaroni and a hot buttered roll and a tiny milk carton and a tan plastic tray before hustling to the gym to get in a quick pickup game before lunch ended. Squeak. Pivot. Squeak. Turn. Squeak.

Shoot.

Squeak.

That sound—the varnish, the squeak of new shoes—was my before.

That sound—my parents crying, the word "oncologist"—was my after.

And nothing would ever be the same again.

CHAPTER TWO

WELCOME TO THE NINTH FLOOR

❖

Oncologist. Never before had one word set off such a firestorm of activity in my typically staid parents. It was as if a fire alarm were going off that just they could hear, sending them scrambling for the exits, only to find them locked and bolted from both sides. There seemed no escape from the word and, worse, the minute they heard it, I realized my poor parents were as trapped as I was.

Turned out Mom and Dad didn't know any oncologists (boy, those were the days), but Mom had a good friend from high school who was working at a hospital in Columbus, so she went home and searched frantically for his number. When she called Dr. Jeffrey Bell that afternoon, she was searching for answers. By the time he called back much later that night, with the wind howling outside and the cold scratching frost against the frozen windowpanes, she had only one question: "Jeff, if your daughters needed an oncologist, who would you recommend?"

Without a second thought, he said, "Dr. Davis."

None of us knew who this mysterious Dr. Davis was—though that was all about to change, and soon—but my mom trusted Jeff entirely, and that was good enough for her. Dr. Davis it would be.

She called the hospital and made arrangements as soon as she got off the phone with Dr. Bell.

I would know none of this until hours later. While Mom and Dad were home talking to Jeff, I was still lying in my cold, sterile bed in Willard Mercy Hospital. I can remember the unmerciful Ohio wind howling right outside my window; its sound seemed to match my mood.

If only I could have howled aloud as well.

I tried to comfort myself with looking around the room, taking note of all the get-well cards, the posters made by the cheerleaders, the balloons from family members, the silent tributes from dozens of caring people who, like me, were helpless to understand the mystery of my condition.

For perhaps the hundredth time that day, I tried to piece together what was going on. What was I doing here? How long would I stay? What was an oncologist? Could he or she help? Would I ever climb again, play basketball, see a movie? Again, exhausted, overwhelmed, my emotions short-circuited from too much introspection, I dozed off into dreamland, joining the howling wind dancing around in my imagination, enjoying, however temporarily, the sweet, blissful release.

Mom and Dad were back in my room, standing patiently at the foot of my bed, by the time dinner arrived. I didn't know how long they'd been there, but it wouldn't have surprised me to find out it had been hours. A growing boy used to six or seven meals a day, not one or two, I couldn't tell which I was happier to see, dinner or my parents. They seemed to understand, waiting a few minutes more while I devoured the bland chicken, lime Jell-O, dark green mushy peas, and a dessert as unnamed as whatever I'd come down with.

When I was done and the empty tray had been cleared away, they told me I was leaving Willard in the morning and that we'd all be heading to Columbus Riverside Methodist Hospital to see this mysterious Dr. Davis. I nodded—more tests—then asked about my brother, Seth. Because he was three years younger, and Mom and Dad wanted to protect him from everything I was going through, he'd been shuffled off to a family friend's house and told we'd call with an update. The news brought another nod from the somber boy in the hospital bed, but I was thinking I couldn't remember the last time we'd spent so many nights apart.

I wondered what he was thinking, if he was enjoying the night away from home, treating it like a slumber party, or losing sleep over what his brother might be going through in the hospital. I figured there was probably a little bit of both going on, and I certainly couldn't blame him. I knew if I'd been in his shoes, I'd have been milking the family intermission for all it was worth.

It stormed so intensely that the next morning, the roads were completely iced over. It was as if Jack Frost had paid us a visit and spit dark, glassy sheets of ice over our entire route, leaving the rest of Ohio unscathed and passable. It took us forty-five minutes to get to the highway, and every single one of them was excruciating.

Dad drove, white-knuckling it the whole way. Mom sat dutifully, silently, beside him, her normally jovial nature drained by four days of not knowing, not sleeping, not eating, not caring what the rest of the world thought about manners or social niceties. I tried to get comfortable on the vinyl of the backseat, my swollen legs propped up on pillows, sliding this way and that and groaning with every bump and grind of the road.

The ninety-mile drive was slick, the family Honda sliding all over the road only to get to a place that was going to cause me more agony than I'd ever imagined in my entire young life. Something was compelling us to get there, but something was also keeping us away. It was as if we were frozen in time; nothing changed.

Mile after mile, nothing was said and nobody moved. Dad's fingers gripped the wheel, Mom's clutched her well-used hand-kerchief, and I struggled to stay still on the shifting backseat. I can't remember if the radio was playing, but I doubt it. I do remember the sound of the tires on the road and our old lives slipping away out the rear window.

I knew where we were going, but I didn't know who'd be coming back. Me? Or some other kid? Some kid with a disease? Some kid with tumors or lumps or bulges or lesions or scabs? I didn't even really know what disease meant back then. All I knew from sickness was what I saw in the horror movies I loved so much, people with faces eaten away from mysterious alien infections or plagues rolling through small midwestern towns, leaving behind nothing but gasping, green-fleshed zombies who would gnaw on your brains and suck on your bones.

I tried to picture my life as a zombie and figured it couldn't be much different from sitting in the backseat of my family's car on this endless, silent, dreary trip. I tried to look for landmarks to help pass the time, but I knew of only one: My grandma lived in Columbus, and I'd ridden there plenty of times with my mom, dad, and Seth. For some reason, this trip seemed to take a lot longer than any other trip we had taken before. I always knew we were getting close to Columbus because there was a barbed-wire fence I saw every time we were about ten miles outside of the city limits.

Shortly after we'd merged onto the highway, I leaned my head against the cold window and kept looking for that fence. Mile after frigid mile passed with little to mark the progress. Snow blanketed the sides of the road, and the flat Ohio landscape lay sullen and pristine outside the foggy car windows.

It was still early, and there weren't that many other cars on the road, but despite the brisk pace and thin traffic, we seemed to be going backward. Where was the damned fence? Finally, it showed up, but instead of taking the normal drive to Grandma's house, we took a different exit. An exit that was completely new to me.

Much like everything else that was about to happen in my life.

The exit led to Riverside Methodist Hospital, where Dad dropped us off at the front of the outpatient door, and Mom and I walked into the building I was about to call my home for the next year. The doctors, the nurses, everyone inside, strangers on this first day, were soon to become my family. It was another before-and-after moment for me, and looking back now, I wonder whether I would have walked through that door if I'd known the horrors that awaited me.

Mom and I walked quietly down the first-floor hallway and turned right into the waiting room, where, as the name implied, people were waiting to be admitted into the hospital. It was a gigantic room (or maybe I was intimidated and felt incredibly small) with those fake, shapeless, portable walls making up about a dozen cubicles where people sat patiently, filling out forms or flipping through outdated copies of *Sports Illustrated, Field & Stream,* and that old waiting-room standby: *Highlights.*

When you walked in, there were chairs to each side in a rough square, separating it from the rest of the room, providing people with a false sense of security because any second your name could be called over the speaker and you'd be the next person sitting on the other side of the table separating the data-entry person and you.

There was a TV on one side of the waiting room, and that's where I was drawn. Anything to take my mind off what was going on. I was thirteen and had no idea what I was getting into. All I knew was that I was sick and we'd had to drive two hours to get to a bigger hospital to find out what was wrong with me, if anything. Part of me believed I'd be dead by sunset; the other figured this was a wild-goose chase and I'd be home by supper, chewing on take-out pizza and being treated like the prodigal son.

What was on TV? What did I watch that day as Mom sat staring at the back of my head and Dad came in from parking the car to sit at her side and clasp her hand as the three of us waited for the door to slam shut on our future? I couldn't tell you. In many ways, I'd already turned into a zombie, staring silently at the screen and disappearing into the flickering images of newscasters or sitcom stars or commercial actors with jock itch or ring around the collar.

Hours could have passed, or only minutes, as I stared at that television set. I suppose one part of my brain was still jacked into reality, because eventually, I heard the familiar squelch of the loudspeaker and then this: "Sean Swarner, number twelve, please. Sean Swarner, please come to cubicle number twelve for registration."

Mom and Dad told me to wait there and they'd take care of everything. I watched them leave, disappearing into a vast honeycomb of cubicles as they wound their way to number twelve, Dad's head barely visible above the top, with Mom's submerged underneath, like a submarine diving for the ocean floor. At some point I lost track of them and turned back to the television.

After a while I got a little anxious and decided to go on an adventure looking for them. I wound through turn after turn, stopping here, starting there, running into a few of the same receptionists more than once and others for the first time. I saw a dozen different coffee mugs with smiley faces and heard the endless clicking of keyboards as people just like me were admitted to what had to be the world's largest and most confusing hospital.

I wondered if they, too, would wind up zombies like me.

After going through the maze of cubicles, I found my parents sitting behind a computer, chatting away with a lady who was safe behind her desk, the owner of yet another smiley-face coffee mug and a plastered-on smile of her own. When I got there, my parents didn't seem too surprised to see me. They had something for me. Something that was going to tell people who I was; something that would be strapped to my wrist every time I came into the hospital again.

I got my new plastic bracelet—name, rank, and serial number, just like the guys on *Hogan's Heroes*—and was told to go sit back down. I stood there, plastic bracelet in hand, puzzled. I'd just spent fifteen minutes trapped like a lab rat in a maze, and now I had to go find my way out? I was such a curious youngster, I wanted to know why I couldn't stay there with Mom and Dad, but they were pretty adamant about it and told me to go sit back down.

Little did I know, they were trying to shelter me from the true reason I was there. Oncology means cancer. Cancer means death.

———

At least that's what everyone thought at that time. My parents included.

When Mom and Dad came back out of their hiding spot to get me, they gently herded me to my room. Our footsteps fell softly on the smooth linoleum, shining back at us with that particular reflective surface that's been glossed to a high sheen by a million midnight moppings after the patients have all gone to sleep. How many times I would lie awake in my room, listening to the swish-wet slapping of that tireless mop, wondering if the old bastard pushing it to and fro knew how lucky he was.

As we turned the corner and entered the elevator single file—Dad first, then Mom, then me—everyone was silent. Whether it was out of deference to the sterile atmosphere of the hospital or that we were buried in our own private thoughts, it seemed like we'd gone far too long without talking. My mom wasn't talking, and that sure wasn't normal. My dad sported a worried look that I had never seen before. Were they turning into zombies, too?

Cocky, I pushed the button number nine so the elevator knew which floor to head to. A floor that would be my home for many years to come. A button I could later find and push with my eyes closed. I touched it so many times, if the crew from *CSI* were to head back there today, I'm sure Grissom or Nick Stokes could still find my fingerprint, or at least some good old DNA still lingering there.

I'll never forget stepping off the elevator onto the ninth floor that day. It was as if the path were already worn into my brain, as if my feet knew just where to go. Instinctively, we turned right and walked into the hallway. The floor was like a small oval track with well-varnished floors, the kind I was introduced to back at Willard. In the center of the track was the nurse's station. Everyone was dressed in blue, looking friendly with constant smiles plastered to their faces; more coffee mugs, more typing fingers.

We found the room. Walked in. Looked around. Surveyed the landscape. True to form, I sat on the bed and instantly started playing with its controls. Up, down, up, down. The former twelve-year-old in me thought it was all a game; my new teenager self somehow knew better but was incapable of acting any more grown up than I'd been the previous year.

Mom pulled the drapes back to reveal soft white snow falling outside, blanketing Olentangy River Road below.

We watched TV while nervously waiting for Dr. Davis. Three pairs of eyes aimed upward at the flickering set, like telescopes trained skyward at the boring old planetarium I went to see on school field trips every year. We were killing time. Even I knew that; waiting it out, sighing, tapping our feet, alternately praying the doctor would get there soon, and hoping he'd never arrive.

It didn't take me long to realize there weren't any good shows on in those half-dozen hospital settings. No matter what I found, it wasn't appealing, and I didn't want to watch it. It could have been my favorite movie at the time, but I still would have constantly flicked the channels. Over and over again, letting out the nervousness and frustration in my flickering fingers. Outside, snow was gently falling. Inside, my family was waiting for one person who would change our lives forever. One person with so much power.

The power to save my life.

About two hours passed, and at last the by now mythical Dr. Davis walked into my room wearing a sterile white lab coat. His presence filled the room, taking up more space than the three of us combined. He had a vibrant red beard, small, round glasses, thinning hair, and, I kid you not, suspenders. I stifled a laugh. The only person I'd ever seen wear suspenders was that Urkel kid on TV. Poor Dr. Davis didn't look much cooler as he strode into the room on the whispering soles of his nondescript Keds.

Instead of introducing himself or shaking my hand, he looked at my mom and asked, "Are you Teri or Jeri?" My mom is a twin, and apparently, both sisters had gone to high school with the man who would become my future doctor. It made me feel a little better, knowing we had a family friend taking care of me.

As Mom would later relate to me, the future Dr. Davis was the president of the chess club and math club back in high school (he was also known as "the chess nerd"). At the moment I didn't care, because the look of respect and relief in Mom's eyes told me that my life was in the hands of a brilliant, brilliant man.

After the introductions, Dr. Davis put his hand on my foot and proceeded to tell us everything he was going to do. He had already ordered a huge battery of tests to begin the next morning. He rattled off a number of different things and used words with five syllables, so, naturally, I was completely lost. Later, he explained in language I could understand.

When he left, I didn't feel better, but at least I felt better informed. I was also exhausted, as were my mom and dad. What had started out as an early-morning odyssey was, incredibly, turning into a snow-filled and darkening evening. There had been so many endless hours—sliding around in the back of the car, sitting in the waiting room, at the cubicle, in my own room waiting for Dr. Davis—that abruptly, the entire day had been eaten up.

The evening passed more quickly than had the day, and somewhere in there I was given a hospital gown and nestled into bed. No more playing with the buttons this time, as the soft, muted tones of the television lulled me into sleep. Mom and Dad hovered close, no doubt gazing down at their helpless little boy, so frail and tired and alone in that big hospital room. I'm sure they kept watch long after I drifted off to sleep.

It was still snowing when we woke up the next morning. Somehow, Mom and Dad must have finagled the hospital staff into letting them sleep in the room with me, Mom on the bed in the room that wasn't occupied and Dad in a La-Z-Boy chair that made a zipping sound every time his clothing rubbed across the fabric. (I'm sure that was comfortable!)

Mom did her best to make it feel like home, drawing the curtains and letting in the snow-dappled sunshine, commenting on the morning news programs as I set a new world record for channel surfing with nervous energy. Mom and Dad revolved through the room as they shuffled downstairs to find hot cups of coffee in the already bustling cafeteria.

Soon a nurse came in, looked at my chart, made a few notations, and roused me from bed, propping me up in a wheelchair she'd brought along and whisking me out of the room toward another long day.

Longer, even. The entire day was full of people wheeling me around in that squeaky wheelchair to different parts of the hospital. Over here for blood work. Over there for X-rays. And my favorite—CAT scans. Not only did they make me drink about four supersize glasses full of what tasted like liquid chalk, but they also poked me and gave me an IV of iodine for good measure. Wonderful stuff that made me hot and tingly all over and even gave me a sensation of peeing myself. (Luckily, it was only a sensation.)

It was also the first time I had major surgery, something as unexpected as it was uncomfortable. Turned out the lymph node on my neck had to be removed to determine what I had and how advanced it was. The X-rays taken that morning had already revealed that this mysterious "it" had spread throughout my lungs. In hindsight, I suppose we should have known something was seriously wrong from that grim news alone. Hope, though, has a funny way of clouding one's perspective.

Looking at the flashes of light seeping through my cloudy X-ray, I remembered going into a biology/science museum with my family the previous summer. (No theme parks or roller coasters for the Swarner family; it was educational or bust, all the way.) The rest of the visit escapes me, but there was this contraption that measured lung capacity. I got the lowest reading in our family. That, too, should have been a sign of something wrong.

Who can trust a museum lung-capacity thingamajig, though, right?

Now here I was in the hospital, getting carted around to every corner of the building, being tested for much more than lung capacity. I felt like I was on another field trip. For a while it was fun, I suppose, because at least I didn't have to walk or do anything but sit there while people pushed me from one place to another. I felt like a king being transported from one country to the next. However, when I finally arrived in that country, the treatment wasn't royal. Vial upon vial of blood was taken out of my frail body. In between, I endured countless pinpricks, stickings, pokings, proddings, temperature checks, X-rays, and CAT scans. All of these things would be considered part of my normal life, and I had to get used to people coming in my room to jab things into my body on a regular basis.

My perspective was purely reactionary; I winced at the pinpricks, groaned at the thermometers, balked at the IVs. It never occurred to me that the blood being whisked away in those endless vials, or the urine or the stool or the saliva or the swabs, might contain clues to the mystery ailment racking my body. I never knew where the vials and tubes and cups went; I didn't care. I didn't want to know what the levels or the facts or the figures or the cells or the counts meant; I didn't want them to mean *anything*. I couldn't picture the studious lab techs in their white coats or the dutiful nurses in their white stockings and shoes as they hunched over microscopes or stuck their noses in petri dishes marked SWARNER, S. I imagined those samples disappearing into the ether, vanishing in the mist that occupied the door outside my hospital room. Inside, I was safe, flicking my channels and playing with the settings on my big, stiff bed; out there, I was poked and mauled like the fattest Boy Scout at a grizzly-bear convention.

I ignored the dozens of people who left the room with pieces of me, and waited for the single person who would come in, smiling, skipping perhaps, and shout, "Eureka, we found the culprit. Sean, by any chance did you swallow a penny when you were a kid? Well, we found it! We've framed it and present it to you now as a souvenir to take home. Home, that's right. *Adios, amigo,* and sorry for all those stool samples!"

If only my parents could have enjoyed the same teenage fantasies that flooded my overtaxed brain. Every time I came out of a room after a test, drained and pale or flushed and trembling, there sat Mom and Dad, both wearing that by-now-familiar worried look on their faces, eyes red from crying. I would look at them and blink until they had composed themselves. I still had no idea what was going on. I knew where I was but not what it meant to *be* where I was. It was all so new to me, and everything was happening way, way too fast for my thirteen-year-old brain to comprehend.

Later that night, I fell into bed, exhausted, drained, and totally spent. I didn't even have enough energy to turn on the TV, let alone flip the channels. My dinner sat cold and uneaten on a yellow plastic partitioned tray, and Mom and Dad took up their respective vigils as I blinked my way deep into a cold, dreamless sleep.

The next day was a white one. Snow was still falling, and the temperature outside was a crisp, bitter cold. You could feel it oozing through the window, and doubly so if you dared to touch your finger to the glass. As we waited for the doctor's report, we watched the early-morning cars trying to maneuver on the ice- and snow-covered highway nine floors below, wondering, guessing aloud where they might be heading and how we'd love to join them, no matter their destination. We joked about the weather and how we would be skiing sometime this winter.

My parents might have been bluffing; I was deadly serious. After all, I thought there was nothing wrong and I'd be out of the hospital in no time. The tubes and vials and cultures and swabs would prove that there was nothing wrong with me after all, and in the end, I'd have the last laugh and everyone would have been just a bunch of silly adults worrying about nothing.

While I was watching TV that morning, after getting used to peeing in the measurement jar (they kept a tab on everything that went in and out of my body), Dr. Davis came through the door requesting that Mom and Dad join him in the hallway. My heart sank, my throat grew dry, my chin quivered. I knew that if the doc couldn't tell me—or didn't want me to know—what was going on in my own body, something had to be terribly wrong.

Suddenly, skiing seemed to be the last thing I'd be doing this winter.

While they were out in the hallway having their private consultation, the news of something known as Hodgkin's disease hit my parents' ears for the first time. I didn't know Mom and Dad knew it was cancer, but I didn't know what it was when they told me. I was almost relieved. After all, at first blush, Hodgkin's disease sounded far better than the dreaded C-word.

Hodgkin's, as I later discovered, is cancer of the lymph system, which protects the body from invasion by things such as bacteria, viruses, fungi, and the like. It basically consists of bone marrow, spleen, tonsils, appendix, and lymph nodes, but I won't go into that too much.

I didn't care, to be honest; I didn't care to see all the way through that looking glass and into the black, startling abyss beyond. All I knew was that I was going to beat it, whatever it was. My parents didn't want to tell me it really *was* cancer just yet, because my step-grandmother had passed away from cancer about a month before I was diagnosed. We'd all watched her endure a particularly grueling battle, and Mom and Dad were trying their best to save me from that association. The next day I was to have another test to see how advanced the disease was.

Dr. Davis lingered in the hall as my parents shared the news with me. I saw him there, skirting the border that separated my room from the hall where he stood. That red beard, those tiny glasses, the suspenders. I loved him and hated him at the same time. I think he'd been around enough diagnoses to know the stages of absorption; he knew my family and I would need time to take it all in, sort it all out, so he stood there patiently, respectfully, there if we needed him but not wanting to intrude on our private grief.

It's an intimate thing, facing words that, no matter how you say them, spin them, dress them up, spell out D-E-A-T-H. Intimate but civil. There we were, politely sitting in my room, the snow swirling outside, Dr. Davis drifting farther and farther into the hall, and Mom and Dad alternately smiling and weeping openly.

We had a lot of time to absorb the diagnosis. All day, in fact. All. Day. We found out that morning and sat there all day. No more tests, no more pokes, no more prods. Nobody came and bothered us; we simply sat there, enduring the agonizing silence of our close, intense, intimate pain. After a few hours, I would have paid one of the nurses passing outside my door to come and stick me with a needle, prop me in a wheelchair, and take me anywhere but that dim, grim room.

Somehow the day passed. Shock has a way of making a minute seem like an hour and two hours seem like a second. Before I knew it, the walls were coated the hazy brown of approaching dusk, and my parents were nibbling on deli sandwiches one of them had drifted down to the cafeteria to bring back up. I drifted in, I drifted out, and I mercifully fell asleep.

I'm certain my poor parents weren't so lucky.

I can still remember waking up to the very large nurses who would perform the "minor surgery" that was to happen in my room the next morning. A bone marrow exam had been scheduled for early in the morning to see if the cancer had made its way into my bone marrow.

The way the test is usually done is the nurses numb up the lower part of your back, right above your butt crack, on both sides. They then proceed to insert this long, thick surgical needle into your skin, past your hipbone and into the actual bone marrow. "Just a little pressure" is what I was told as they quickly applied the anesthetic and prepped me for the procedure.

"You won't feel a thing," they said. "Any pain is just pressure, and it'll go away when we're done."

They sounded so convincing, so sincere.

Go away, my ass. How can you tell me that it's not going to hurt, shoving a needle past *bone?* I can't even imagine how much pressure and strength you need to shove steel past bone and then to be careful enough not to blast through the bone marrow and shatter the other side of the bone.

No wonder those nurses were so big.

"You won't feel a thing, Sean." I'll never forget those words, because nothing could have been further from the truth. The nurse numbed my lower back, and while she was waiting for that to take effect, another nurse came up to the right side of the bed. I was lying on my stomach, and she took my right hand in hers and told me that if I needed to, I could squeeze her hand if it hurt.

I thought of all the old Westerns I'd watched where the side-kick told the wounded hero to bite the bullet while some wild-haired and half-drunk prairie doc dug buckshot out of his hindquarters or sawed off his big toe. Somehow I knew I'd never look at John Wayne the same way again.

"Here we go," said the nurse with the straw-sized steel needle. "You're just going to feel a little prick," she added as she started driving the steel into my lower back. Squeezing the other nurse's hand, I said through teary eyes that I could feel every-thing she was doing back there and I was in excruciating pain.

"It's just the pressure," they both continued to tell me, lying in concert.

Once again I told her how much pain I was in and suggested they should wait longer because the Novocain hadn't had time to start working, and I was in so . . . much . . . pain. They ignored me, and soon I was squeezing the nurse's hand so hard that she put my hand on the bed frame so I didn't crush her hand any more than I had already. I gripped the bed frame so hard, I was surprised not to hear the sound of crushing metal.

To describe pain so intense requires words I do not possess, words that perhaps the entire English language doesn't possess. Up until then, pain was a stubbed toe or scraped knee, a rug burn from roughhousing on the new carpet in the den or a titty twister from one of my friends at the bus stop.

This was a new level of pain, something novel and unique to my teenage experience. "Searing" is not the right word; the steel slid through my flesh slowly, dragging with it nerve endings that jangled and screamed for mercy. A pinprick was quick, sharp, and over before you knew it. Out of necessity, however, this proce-dure was agonizingly slow. The so-called pressure had to be just right, not too hard, not too fast, not too far, not too short.

I could see the skin of my hand gone pale; feel the sweat bead and drip off my forehead. Seconds stretched into days, and the world stopped on a dime. All that existed was the pain, and it would not go *away*. It radiated out, then throbbed back in, col-lapsing on itself and burning anew as, centimeter by centimeter, more steel gouged the virgin flesh of my bleeding backside.

All of a sudden the nurse playing with the torture device

stopped. She said they were done with that one. The words sent a fresh shiver of pure, unadulterated fear up my spine. I wanted to run away, to scream, but was too weak to do either. Unfortunately, they had aspirated a piece of bone and not marrow. The nurse told me they would have to do it not once more but *twice* more. My mom was no longer in the room because she couldn't bear to see her son in so much agonizing pain. Although I'd been too delirious to realize it, she had left the instant they started sliding the steel past my skin.

As much as I wish I could forget this experience, it's burned into my memory as if it happened yesterday. I can still feel the pain shooting up my back and reaching my brain as I lay there trying to convince the nurses that what I felt was pain and not pressure.

The second time was even worse than the first, if only because I knew what was coming and how much it would hurt. My nerve endings learned quickly, shrieking against the pain even before the steel met flesh. Where the needle had pierced the bone before was raw and tender, exposed and vulnerable, as once again the needle plucked at parts of my body never meant to be touched.

By the third time she inserted the steel-bladed syringe into my skin, I was floating in and out of consciousness from the pain. Eventually, it was over. I passed out, and my mom came into the room to see how things had gone. Needless to say, I hope I never have to have another one of those again. To this day, I have three little scars above my butt that'll never go away, grim reminders of my first clash with the torture devices of modern medicine.

I wish I could say that day was complete, but later that afternoon, I was scheduled to have a Hickman catheter placed in my chest. A Hickman catheter is basically a permanent IV that protrudes out of your chest about eight inches (coiled up and taped to the chest when not in use), works its way under the skin, over the clavicle, and into a major vein in the neck. From there it goes directly to the heart to circulate the chemotherapy over the entire body. It's a convenience that I'd never take for granted after going through all the treatments, that's for certain.

Though I'd only just recovered from that morning's trauma, the "chauffeurs" came to pick me up from my room and wheel me down to the operating room. Lucky for me, I never had to leave my bed to get into a wheelchair, because the bed had wheels on it.

I got to the operating room and thought everything after the bone marrow test would be downhill. I was completely wrong. The surgery didn't hurt one bit, because I was knocked out cold; however, the transfer from my bed to the operating table was nothing short of excruciating.

They lifted me up by the small of my back, placing their hands and arms directly on the spot where I'd had the procedure earlier that day. My eyes filled, and tears flowed down my cheeks. There was no control, no pride, no shame, no time for thought. I couldn't even talk to tell them what was wrong. All I could stammer was a weak and whimpering "b-b-bone marrow." They understood exactly what was wrong, immediately put me down, and picked me up using the bedsheet like a tarp. The rest of the surgery, like I said, was cake. I don't remember a thing, and I think I even had some pretty cool dreams, none of which had anything to do with steel or pipe or needles or straws.

Waking up back in my room, I noticed I had these things connected to my body. The tube hanging out of my chest was attached to what would be known soon as "my buddy." The IV pole was adorned like a Christmas tree with many different bags marked "radioactive."

Even as I lay there, weak and wounded, stunned and staid, the chemotherapy was coursing through my body. It wasn't centralized, it was everywhere. I had been wrong: I wasn't a zombie after all. Instead, I was a radioactive cyborg, living off pumps and dials, hooked up to wires and machines, about to embark on a life-changing journey and learn more about living than most people would ever want to endure without first begging to die. I was the star of my own horror movie come to life, a modern-day Frankenstein pieced and patched together, still leaking from the holes poked and peeled from my body.

I wondered if the kids back home would recognize me, wondered if I'd ever make it back home. Or would they shrink back and cover their eyes, hiding from the monster their friend had become, shielding themselves from the reality of the human body gone awry.

CHAPTER THREE

IMMOBILE

❖

I don't remember much of my first treatment, but slowly, things are coming back to me. My brain is bringing into my consciousness what my body and mind went through that first week in the hospital. I suppose it's the body's defense mechanism, shutting down certain parts of the mind so we can endure the unendurable.

The first round of chemo took a toll on my family and me. Today it's uncommon to find someone who doesn't know what chemo is like; back then, in the late 1980s, you didn't know what to expect until you'd lived through it—some might say died and come back through it. Perhaps it was better that way: If I'd known what I was in store for, I might never have gone through with it in the first place.

Right before the chemo started, I received a care package from my aunt. Among the various cookies and treats and get-well sentiments was a little stuffed animal. One of those annoying ones with eyes and a nose that blink and beep every time you touch it, clap, or make so much as a tiny noise. Annoying, right? Well, not when you're hopped up on some good drugs. At the time I thought it was the coolest thing in the world.

The drugs made me feel like an astronaut. The joystick that made my hospital bed go up and down became the controls of the spaceship, and the noisy little creature was my space-bound companion, my copilot in this grand adventure fueled by my mind, streamlined by the Ativan and other anti-nausea drugs, endured by my parents, who had a ringside seat to their son's outer-space excursion into delirium.

All at once the bed shook, and my body pressed against the mattress from the force of the engines blasting my noisy copilot and me into outer space. The entire ride through the earth's atmosphere, the light brown creature in a blue hooded overcoat constantly giving me directions and navigational information.

Laughing at me. His beady eyes looking at me and blinking white light every time we moved, his glowing, twitching nose matching the unspoken conversation we were having: "Pilot to copilot. Warp speed terminated. Missiles armed. Enemy engaged. Fire! Fire! Fire!" His stitched mouth never once opened, but I understood him completely. He was hysterical; I was invincible; the world of needles and marrow and cancer and chemo and hospitals was far beneath us, disappearing with every hollow laugh or move of the joystick.

All the way up through the atmosphere and through the vacant nothingness of space, he and I laughed our way into purposeful oblivion. Never mind that we didn't have any oxygen to breathe up there because my body was safe in the hospital bed with the rails up to protect me. My mind was a million miles away. Eventually, my little friend and I landed on the moon and went for a walk on the rocky surface.

Still giggling like schoolgirls in our space helmets, we roamed the cratered surface of the moon, discovering different caves and checking out all the cool rocks. He told me he used to live here and this was his home. When we got tired and wanted to head back to earth, we managed our way back to the space shuttle to head home.

For me, it was fantastic—a temporary escape from the insanity that had become my earthbound life. For my family, in the room seeing what this drug did to me, the experience was nearly impossible to deal with: a high-pitched, childish laugh for over four hours straight.

Years later, my mom shared with me her journal entries of those troubling first few days of chemo treatment. I shuddered with horror as I read what she wrote.

Wednesday, February 3

Riverside Hospital. 1st chemo treatment. Ativan medication. Ativan—laughing for hours. Trips to moon and back. Like a drunk. He was flying. Treatment about 1 P.M. Infantile behavior and high-pitched laughs for 4 hours. I could hardly stand it. We put sides up on bed thought he'd "fly" out of there. Difficult to see your child given drugs to make him do that. This stuff to get well? Foreign med and then this . . . vomiting. Weds, Thursday changed bed 4 times. Weds I just got sheets and changed it. Nurses so good. Jennifer and string games.

Thursday, February 4

Riverside. Vomiting. Not much food. Pizza—late P.M.

Friday, February 5

Riverside. Eating well. Release before dinner. We went out but decided not to eat much. Sean only ate part of his meal. I guess he overdid it before.

Imagine someone you love with all of your heart, an otherwise intelligent, bright person who, because of some insignificant anti-nausea medication, has been reduced to a sniveling infant with no cognitive abilities whatsoever. A worthless, unintelligent, uncomprehending newborn shoved into the unwilling, unresponsive, unprepared body of a thirteen-year-old. And it was imperative that this person go through all of this to get better. Was it worth it? Yes. Was it easy? No.

Hell, no.

The first round of chemotherapy treatments was horrible. They started the toxic medicinal IV drip into my newly placed Hickman catheter just after one P.M., when I woke up and saw myself attached to all these gadgets and tubes coming out of my body. (Maybe I had gone to the moon after all!) Within hours I was vomiting nonstop. What went down came right back up. There was no controlling it, no stopping it.

In forty-eight short hours, the nurses had changed the linens on my bed four times because of the puking and the incontinence. Countless trips to the bathroom when I didn't make it, or when I couldn't physically get out of bed because I was so drained and in so much pain, made my room a jungle of strange, unendurable noises, colors, and smells.

I'll never forget crawling on my hands and knees, trying to make it to the toilet to vomit in there and not all over myself or the bed or the floor or whatever was near—a cup, the bedpan, a trash can, whatever. After the trip to the moon, I crash-landed back to reality, harder and uglier than ever. Once the drug wore off, things were obviously miserable.

I'd always been shy and self-conscious about such things and was doubly so as a fresh-faced, naive teenager. My appearance, my naked body, my private moments were sacrosanct, and now I was reduced to a quivering, giggling, vomiting, oozing wreck, at the beck and call of nurses and doctors who knew every inch of my body intimately. To pass out halfway between my bed and the bathroom in a pile, a puddle, of my own making would have been horrifying only a week earlier; now it was par for the course. Such is one of the unspoken side effects of chemo.

It seemed like the doctors didn't know any more about what to do with me than my family did. Basically, the hospital made a concoction of medicine to see what my body could handle. Obviously, this was not the right mixture for a healthy recovery, and the doctors and nurses needed to experiment with some different juices to stop my body and mind from going crazy.

I was in the hospital for about five days before they let me out. The whole time they were monitoring everything and keeping an eye on my intake and output. Liquids, solids, juice, meat, even ice cubes, in or out, had to be carefully recorded and analytically examined. I had a chart outside the bathroom where I had to keep track of when I went "number two," as they called it, or even when I peed. When I actually did pee, I had to go in a jar that looked like a big see-through plastic beer mug with measurements on the side.

I'd walk outside the bathroom and write down how much I had. Before I was allowed to do it on my own, however, I needed to let the nurses know every time I went to the toilet so they could dutifully record my number one or two. How embarrassing—teenager having to tell some strange lady that he just took a leak or a dump, *and* how much of it there was! I wanted to crawl into a hole and never come out.

What made the first treatment tolerable were the people who surrounded me. You never know how precious your loved ones can be until the carpet is ripped out from under you and you see who's standing there to pick you up again.

Some were well known and familiar to me, others were strangers one minute and best friends and allies the next. My family, the nurses, the doctor, friends, and the occasional cute candy striper. One nurse in particular took me under her wing. We played string games practically every day to pass the time. You know the type—cat's cradle, butterfly, the Eiffel Tower, that kind of thing.

Dr. Davis also came in quite often to check up on me, sit next to me, and see how things were going. He was only thirty-six years old at the time, but he seemed years older, with his thinning hair, thick glasses, pink shirts, and suspenders. Though his appearance might have been stern, his attitude was upbeat, young, and accessible. He called me "friend" in a soft, comforting voice.

A lot of the experience was hazy for me—the moon shot, the stuffed animal, the nausea, the trips to the bathroom—but I do remember Dr. Davis constantly asking me questions about how I was feeling, if I needed anything, telling me about the treatments and why they made me feel like I did. He was incredible.

No matter what I asked him, how silly or serious, limited or lame, he answered me with the concern and compassion of a true professional. He spoke to me one-on-one, in a way that made the hospital seem more warm and alive. He was more than just a doctor to me. Since I was away from the routine and rut of school, he became my teacher. When my parents were as scared and uncertain as I was, he became my father figure. When I was depressed, he became my cheerleader. When I was lonely, he became my friend.

He was always sharing his huge deli cookies with me, too. "Here, friend," he'd say after a quick trip downstairs to the cafeteria, "eat it. It's good for you. It's part of the treatment," he'd add with a wink, one hand bearing a huge cookie and the other clutching one of his suspenders. Too bad it didn't stay down long. It tasted much better the first time around, that's for sure.

As hard as this first treatment was on me, I did all I could to help those around me. Through the haze of drugs and fear and nausea and sleeplessness, I tried to let Mom and Dad know that I was okay. I was going to be fine. I knew it was going to be a long process and a long time battling whatever it was I had, which I still didn't fully comprehend or understand or, at this point, even have a name for. It didn't quite matter, because I knew whatever it was, I was going to beat it.

Weeks later, when they had evened out my chemo regimen and I was able to move around freely, I found out I had the horrible disease, cancer, when I went to the hospital library and did some research on Hodgkin's disease. Regardless, I tried telling my family that I would be fine without them if they wanted to go home or if they wanted to get something to eat, or even if they wanted some rest from the constant in-and-out of the hospital room.

We think of hospital rooms as calm, quiet, stale places where a patient lies in a bed and the family waits and waits and waits. Not my room; it was more like Grand Central Station, with people coming in and out all hours of the day and night to monitor my blood pressure, temperature, intake, output. It was a constant zoo or, more appropriately, an ant farm of drones doing their jobs.

In other words, keeping me alive.

Apparently, the nurses really liked me because they were so used to older people battling cancer and never any younger people. I was put on an adult floor because there weren't children's wards or floors just for kids back when I was battling cancer. It was strange, because whenever I had the motivation and energy to walk around the hallways, all I saw were older people attached to their "little buddies" (IV poles) and sleeping.

My attitude was a great change of pace for the nurses. They would go back to the nurses' station and say, "Did you see the good-looking young boy in room 9020?"

My life became a battle of extremes. When I was bad, I was very bad. Laughing, giddy, silly, throwing up, unrecognizable. When I was good, it was as if nothing had happened, as if I weren't in the hospital at all but on some extended vacation where everyone waited on me and cute nurses coddled me. On these days I was my old self, playing practical jokes and making up goofy names for the candy stripers or joking with the local family friends who frequently stopped by for a visit.

One day after the nurses left and we were alone, my mom looked at me and asked, "Sean, do you ever ask yourself how you joke about all this?"

I thought about that for a minute, and then I told her, "I don't ask, 'Why me?' or 'Why not Seth or Andy or any of my other friends?' anymore. No one knows why I got it, and I accept that. I just say, 'I've got it, and now I'm going to get rid of it.' What else can I do, Mom?"

She had no answer for me, but I frequently look back on that conversation and what it meant to us both. So often the survival is dictated by the survivor. I've talked to many people who've overcome cancer, and we all respond differently. Some become more extroverted, others draw inward. Some go through the five stages of coping with death as if it's a foregone conclusion; others become daredevils, addicts, or act out in ways they never before imagined.

From the beginning, a switch went off in my head. There was my body, and then there was my mind; not one and the same but two different entities. This disease, this Hodgkin's, this cancer, could eat away at my body, pull out all my hair, reject every bite of pizza I ate or glass of milk I drank, but it couldn't get inside my head. When it got too bad, I'd go to the moon or revisit one of my childhood memories or make plans for the future.

I don't know if the cancer forced me to grow up early or if the disease merely magnified various personal traits I already harbored and would have grown into anyway, but my decision was black and white, never gray: I would survive; the cancer wouldn't.

Would I ever have climbed a mountain if I hadn't gotten the cancer? Probably. Would climbing a mountain mean more to me after surviving cancer? You bet. Recording your daily urine output or throwing up your favorite meal or pulling out clumps of your own hair in the shower is not only a great motivator, it's the ultimate validation of life and all its many possibilities.

Even as I endured the tests and the poking and the prodding and the puking, I knew I would never be the same little boy again. Childhood was over; adulthood had begun. I was forced to grow up.

About five days after my first chemo treatment, I was put into a wheelchair and moved from my room to the front door of the hospital. I thought I was in for another round of tests or, perhaps, horror of horrors, some more bone marrow torture sessions; instead, I was being released.

I said a quick goodbye to my favorite doctors and nurses and orderlies and candy stripers, but I knew it wasn't farewell. I'd be back soon enough; we all knew it.

What was in store for me would be some difficult trips in and out of the hospital. There was nothing routine or habitual about it; my schedule would never be the same, because it all depended on my blood counts, my vital stats, and how I was feeling that day. There would be times when I was in school for a couple of classes for a few days in a row, then drop off the radar. I would disappear from school to be in the hospital for a week, then reappear as if nothing had happened.

On our way home that first time, we stopped at a restaurant to get some nonhospital food, but my big night out was short-lived and underfed; I could stomach only part of the meal. That was a change from someone who usually scarfed down his entire meal and was always a member of the clean-plate club.

Once I was home and situated, life took on a semblance of routine. I was back in my own bed, my own room, wearing my own clothes, and looking at my own things. Mom cooked all my favorite foods, and I started eating and keeping food down again.

Now would begin the transition back into school and classes after being in the hospital for what seemed like months but was probably more like three weeks. Time took on a malleable quality; hours could feel like days, and days could pass like minutes. I stopped thinking in terms of classes or days or hours and rationed out my time on earth in vials and tubes and hospital visits.

At any rate, the typical teenage questions were, at the very least, a distraction from the treatment and the adjustment back into "civilian" life: Would my teachers make a big fuss about my return? Would the girls still think I was cute? Would my friends still like me? What would they do? How would they react? Regardless, I was out of the hospital, and I think this was the first time in my life I was actually anxious to get back to school.

I didn't look any different—yet. That was all about to change. Refining the chemo meant less nausea and vomiting (better meds and anti-nausea drugs didn't hurt), but more long-lasting and visible changes were still on the way. So were a lot of traumatic events that I was neither prepared for nor able to handle very well, let alone control.

I started avoiding showers because I got tired of looking down at the drain and seeing more and more of my hair swirl down the drain along with my soap and shampoo. Combing my hair became daily torture; the more I combed, the more I lost. The more I lost, the more I knew the kids at school would notice. The more they noticed, the harder things got for me. It got so I never wanted to see another comb, brush, or mirror again.

To make matters worse, the drugs I was taking had another side effect: I was gaining weight. For me, weight had never been a problem. I was active, growing, frenetic; I could down three plates of anything, and it barely made a dent. An hour later, I was hungry again. When we shopped for school, it was because I'd grown up, not out. Now I was looking in the men's department to find pants that would fit. What was next? The Big and Tall store?

I couldn't believe how much my life had changed, practically overnight, and adjusting to the changes—physical, emotional, spiritual—was a constant struggle. I'd been the cute kid in room 9020 a few weeks ago in the hospital. Now I was the hairless freak who couldn't stop gaining weight. My cheeks got puffy, my belly ballooned, everything swelled in all the wrong places at just the wrong time.

My hair was thinning, falling out in clumps—I looked more and more like Dr. Davis every day, and once I even wore suspenders to keep up my pants in his honor. One day I visited the hospital for a checkup, and Dr. Davis patted me on the head out of habit. "Hey, friend, how's it going?" he asked, per usual.

I immediately shrank back and told him, "Doc, watch the head. I need all the hair I can save!" We laughed about it, but my appearance was becoming more and more of a concern, and nothing anybody said about it helped. It was like I was having a midlife crisis, looking in the mirror for minutes at a time and trying to pinpoint where I'd lost the most hair and where it might disappear next.

It was still winter in Ohio, and every morning I'd slick my hair to one side or the other, depending on which side needed more cover, and hope for only a light breeze. Before I knew it, there were only a few strands left; I looked like my grandpa! It was like a glimpse into the future: Now at least I knew what I'd look like when I turned seventy-five. Meanwhile, my parents were looking for wig makers, presenting the idea a little at a time, a quick mention at breakfast, a question or two at dinner, until at last it didn't seem so ridiculous after all.

Looking back over this, it all sounds so neat and clipped, but at the time, life moved in inches and minutes, few of them pleasant and many of them torturous, merciless, and bordering on the obscene. I was in the eighth grade, losing my hair and gaining weight from the medicine. Being that young is a popularity contest, and for once in my life, I wasn't winning anything.

It was my first year as a teen. My world shrank to my mirror and my closet. What would I look like today? What would I wear? World events, politics, the box office, the Billboard charts, homework, grades, none of it really mattered anymore. All I cared about was that people understood why I looked as I did. I didn't care what they thought; it just concerned me that they could comprehend why a thirteen-year-old was chunky and bald. A smile in the hall could send me soaring on cloud nine. A frown, a whisper, a pointed finger, a hand cupped to hide a snicker, any or all of these could send me despondent and shuffling to my next class, where I would sit watching the clock and waiting for the day to end.

It was so frustrating. I had neither the words nor the maturity to deal with being ostracized. It was so sudden, so subjective. How could I make them understand this was all temporary? Why couldn't they see that this new, fleeting me—the bad skin, zero hair, bloated flesh, shrunken eyes—wasn't the old me, wasn't the *real* me?

I didn't necessarily become self-conscious, but more aware of how powerful other people's thoughts and gestures could be to my own fragile psyche. A loving family, a little brother who looked up to me, friends who stuck by me through thick and thin: These things had given me more than enough confidence to skate by on for as long as I could remember. Now none of that mattered. Suddenly, it was me trying to deal with people's stares, hidden glances, and strange looks.

Few things are more important to a thirteen-year-old boy than girls, but to me they were abruptly inconsequential. Looks, status, and popularity were all that mattered to the pretty, popular, perky girls I was most attracted to. All at once I had none of the above. I'd been on the cusp of becoming a handsome young man; now I felt like a troll waddling out from beneath his bridge each morning, head shiny, thighs rubbing together, in ill-fitting clothes, and avoiding the sunlight.

My friends grew and matured. They got tougher, taller, stronger while I got balder, paler, fatter, weaker. They could wear the popular styles and stay active; they looked like thirteen-year-old boys looked, and the girls were noticing how they looked.

More than the disease itself, the side effects were what bummed me out the most during this all-important time in my life. Being a teenager is never easy; going to school in clothes that didn't fit, sucking in my puffy cheeks while I combed over my last few strands of hair, I wanted to shrink into the walls and become invisible.

I'd always been a loud, boisterous, fun-loving kid. Life was recess, basketball, swimming, goofing on substitute teachers, and flirting with the new girl. I lived for those few carefree moments between class, cutting up and knocking around with my friends. I still had my diehard buddies, my loyal friends who'd known me from day one and would be there until the end of days, but when they weren't around, my life was lonely, sad, scared, and dull.

The cool table in the cafeteria had been my domain for as long as I could remember. Now I had a hard time getting the nerds to let me sit with them. Even today my palms get sweaty writing this; I don't know how I dragged myself out of bed and went in there every day, but somehow I managed. It didn't help that most people didn't know what I had or why I looked the way I did. What hurt worse was how few of them cared.

Since my family, friends, and I never really used the C-word, and "Hodgkin's" sounded so mysterious and foreign, I think it was easier for everyone to goof on, point at, or simply ignore me. It got so bad that sometimes I longed for that first week in the hospital; at least there no one judged me, not even when I was puking or making marks on my pee chart.

Hair or no hair, weight or no weight, life went on, such as it was. Nothing was ever neat and clean; there was no easy triumph or closure. I'd get comfortable in some new routine and then have to go back to the hospital for another round of treatments. I'd be drifting off to sleep after a restless night of nausea and tossing and turning, and it would be time for school. I'd get used to combing my hair this way, and a new clump would mean I'd have to find an alternate hairstyle. Every day was an end to something and a beginning to something else.

The anti-nausea drugs took time to be effective, and they didn't always work. I'd be fine at dinner, overconfident and over-compensating, and then hurling for two hours at four in the morning. My parents slept little and were always on high alert; they'd hear me retching, and one or the other would come run-ning to pat me on the back when it was all over or offer me a cold compress for my head.

My little brother, Seth, was so good: He'd be patient with me even when I was having a tantrum or being impatient about something inconsequential or otherwise stupid. I know my par-ents tried not to let my sickness rob Seth of his own childhood, giving him special Seth time and making sure his needs were al-ways validated, but I'm sure he lost a part of his own childhood while I suffered through mine. At times I still feel guilty for pulling him through it and not letting him have a "normal" child-hood, like everyone deserves.

School continued to be a thorn in my side, but once I got used to playing on the bench, it was not as bad as I'd feared. My friends understood and, despite a few awkward moments at first, quickly got used to seeing me with bald spots and comb-overs and zombie skin and bags under my eyes. At first I tried to keep up with track or soccer practice, but I'd missed a big chunk of time, and it got harder and harder adjusting to the weight gain, frequent nausea, and lack of sleep.

School suffered, too. I would go for the first two periods and then have to come home, or go for the last two periods and scramble to get my makeup work from the first four. Teachers, counselors, coaches, and most of all my friends understood. I was still Sean; I just looked different.

I think in many ways, they were as relieved to see me as I was to see them. They'd heard so many rumors from the grapevine—Sean was dying, Sean was dead, Sean lost his leg, Sean was never coming back to school—that to see me must have been like seeing a ghost.

I laughed as much as I could, joking and razzing and goofing and playing. I overdid it a lot, I know. Running too much in PE, eating too much at lunch, forgetting the rules Dr. Davis had given me or even my own good instincts, and paying later with swollen joints or sore muscles or time hunched over the porcelain God, my new bestest friend. I couldn't help it. My friends were like sunshine that bone-frigid winter. I tried to soak up as much of them as I could, whenever I could.

It did bum me out to miss school, believe it or not. Anything to get out of that bedroom, that house, that bathroom, to see new people or feel normal for a few hours a day or live up to the challenge of flirting—without hair.

When my wig finally arrived, I didn't know whether to laugh

or cry, so I did both. It seemed a little light in color for me, not much like my old hair at all. It looked too old for me also, like something you'd see on a nursing home resident or game show host. Mom said they could dye it darker later, but to try it on for a fit. I did. It was scratchy, stiff, and uncomfortable. I'd lost all perspective about how I looked; the mirror lied so often, I no longer trusted it.

My friend Andy happened to come by that day for a visit, and despite our lifelong friendship, it took everything I had to try on the wig in front of him. "Does it look real?" I asked him after a few awkward moments.

He stared at the ground and nodded. Then he looked me right in the eyes and lied. "Sure," he said. "I can barely tell."

It was a moment trapped in time, frozen in my memory. I knew in an instant that my hair didn't matter, that having no hair didn't matter, that wearing a wig didn't matter. Friends, family, doctors, nurses—people—*they* were all that mattered.

CHAPTER FOUR

REALITY CHECK

❖

So began the regimen of treatments, the endless procession in and out of the hospital, the to-and-fro of health and weakness, weakness and health. It felt strange to make the horrific so mundane. Without much effort or forethought, taking a trip to the hospital fell right into the rest of our daily routines. In no time, our days were filled with carpools and playdates and extracurricular activities and, oh yeah, time for Sean's chemo! Many was the time my mother threatened to change her family title from "Soccer Mom" to "Dr. Mom." (On our more morbid days, Mom and I dared to suggest she get a bumper sticker that, instead of MOM'S TAXI, would read the more appropriate MOM'S AMBULANCE.)

I'd go into the hospital for a day, get the treatments, and ride home, sitting like a limp rag in the backseat, feeling pale and discarded and looking twice that bad. I'd recover at home until I had to head back for round two of the cycle. This phase was the worst of the two; it meant a few days in the hospital for the IV drip, and then I'd go back home, even more washed out than the first time, dreading the routinely inevitable.

After I got back to Willard from the daylong inpatient treatments, I'd usually start vomiting at four A.M. It was like clockwork; later, Mom would joke that she could have set her watch by it, but of course, it was no laughing matter. Not to me, anyway. Vomiting continuously from Wednesday morning until Friday afternoon became my end-of-the-week routine. Jell-O, ice cream, even water came right back up.

They weren't the only things: It was a struggle to keep even the anti-nausea pills down. At this point, what did it matter? *Everything* came back up. All day long, for twelve hours straight, I alternated between lying in bed and running to the bathroom to puke. Most times I made it; others times I didn't. It was a relentless, vicious cycle. Regurgitation became a way of life.

The few times I'd thrown up before chemo had been occasions for relief, not quite misery. A flu bug that vomiting helped get rid of, a few too many hot dogs or bags of cotton candy at the annual carnival, a quick retch or two behind the Tilt-A-Whirl, and all was right with the world. "Hey, Mom, can I have two dollars for a candy apple?" This wasn't like that. Half the time there wasn't anything left to throw up, and the other half, what came back up were food and nutrients my body sorely needed. Throughout it all, at least I was getting a good abdominal workout.

Beyond the physical act of retching followed a host of other ills, including the perpetual scent of vomit that lingered along my path from bathroom to bed; the ever present taste of that morning's meal on the roof of my mouth, in my nostrils, and on my sleeve; an aching back and red splotches on my knees from hovering over the porcelain god; and a sore and burning throat most days of the week.

As one might imagine, I started getting tired from (and of) the treatments. The human body can take only so much, and even at my then-tender age, the powers of recovery are put to the test when the body is in constant physical turmoil. I was watching a documentary not long ago about one of my favorite subjects— mountains, natch—and how sedimentary layers build up over time. They compared the disruptions in these layers to the rings in a tree trunk, how in times of drought or intense weather or geographic change, the rings, the layers, are thinner than during times of plentiful water, food, and nourishment.

In the sedimentary layers of my life, that was a pretty thin year.

It sounds strange to say it, but at least the nausea was predictable, and when your life is turned upside down, even the painfully predictable can be seen as safe. The nausea no longer scared me. Don't get me wrong, it was nasty and painful and a royal pain, but I wasn't scared of it anymore. What scared me the most were the surprises: the pains and ills and side effects that came out of nowhere and spun my life in yet another direction like a spoiled kid picking up a perfectly good top and spinning it all over again.

Case in point: I had some incredibly strange and painful things happen to a region south of my fading hairline—my eyes. The first time it happened was one of the scariest moments of my life. I was completely out of control and unable to do anything about it. It was like being blind while still being able to see; all that was visible was the ceiling, the roof, whatever was above me.

To this day I have the fear that my eyes are going to do this and I'm going to lose control. I know it's ridiculous to think this way after so many years, but it had such an impact on me that I still think about it.

It started out like any other day. Any other Sean Swarner day, that is. Mom was driving me from lunch to the hospital for more treatments when it started. I vividly remember sitting in the car, turning left to look at something we were passing, and my eyes felt like they were drifting up. Slowly, slowly upward. Higher and higher, and there was nothing I could do about it. It was horrible. I thought the hair and the nausea and the vomiting and the weight gain was bad—then this.

I tried looking down, but that made things worse. Mom parked in a handicapped spot in the parking garage and took me by the arm to help me walk up to the hospital floor and the doc's office. I walked down the hallway, looking up at the lights and seeing only what was directly above me. It wasn't much, because most of my pupils were under my upper eyelids.

Because it was involuntary, my neck started to strain from behind, and my head went back as well. I tried to pull it down, but it was nearly impossible. It was like being on a ride at the fair, where the feeling of gravity is induced and you are no longer able to control your extremities. It was completely out of my control, no matter what I did to stop it. To make matters worse, I was wearing gas permeable contacts (basically like hard contacts, circa the mid-80s), and I couldn't get them out of my eyes. I honestly thought I was going blind, and I couldn't stop worrying about my eyes rolling into my head permanently. I remember saying to my mom, "I'm walking on the ceiling—I'm seeing things! Mom, help me, please make it stop. I can't stand it."

When we got into the doctor's office, the nurses gave me a muscle relaxant to calm me down. My eyes slowly started to relax and focus again on what was in front of me and not above my head. Turned out I had been experiencing an allergic, muscular reaction to the medicine. I decided on the spot, right then and there, that I wasn't going to take any more anti-nausea medicine, and I was never going to get sick again. (Unfortunately, that wasn't the case—I ended up taking a mild anti-nausea medication because I did get sick again.)

As you can imagine, by this time I was getting tired of everything going wrong. Of battling this disease and fighting for my life on a daily basis. Adults have a hard time handling this; how was I supposed to do it when I was just a kid? I was supposed to be worrying about soccer practice and reaching puberty, who to ask to the fall dance or how close to sit to my dream girl in the movie theater. Kid things, normal things, teen things. The things my friends were worried about. I never resented them, by the way. My friends. I only wanted it to be over with. I wanted it to end. Now, instead of ending, it seemed to be ramping up.

The eye rolling signaled a shift in my treatments. I'd just come to terms with constant nausea and daily vomiting, and the fear of losing my sight—even temporarily—took its toll on my frame of mind. I couldn't sleep for long periods because I was constantly vomiting and constantly afraid of having my eyes roll back into my head. I was sick of it, to be honest. I didn't know if it was worth it anymore, I really didn't, but still, somehow, I managed to hold on. Through it all, I believed that I had a long life in front of me and did my best to enjoy every day I woke up because it was a true gift. What's that saying? "Every day aboveground is a good day." That's truly how I felt back then, and even now.

Every time I went into the hospital for a treatment, I'd always be put on the ninth floor. It was like my home away from home, a safe haven from the unknowns that dotted the outside world. I knew every corner of that floor like the back of my hand. Which water fountain had the coldest water, which waiting room had the biggest TV, which wheelchair had the quietest wheels. The nurses, doctors, and other staff members who worked there became my family. It's hard not to get to know people when you see them twice a week, every week.

It was comforting going in and recognizing every face on the ninth floor, until that fateful day when I was checked in to another floor in the hospital. New nurses, new faces, new beds, new everything. I was depressed and didn't want to be there. I was worried things weren't going to come out well and I was going to be violently ill, that the shift in floors was a bad omen, a jinx on my recovery.

Fortunately, the hospital staff knew I was supposed to be on the ninth floor, and they were doing everything they could to get me up there, but all the beds were taken, and I had to stay on a lower floor—the doomed, jinxed floor—until another bed opened. When one finally did, the interns instantly wheeled me up into the new room and put me in the new bed. It was a single room, so there were no green curtains separating one bed from another. It was just me, as if I'd been somehow rewarded for enduring my temporary exile on what would later become known as "the floor below."

My "normal" floor, my "normal" nurses. At last I could breathe easy again. Everyone was smiling when they saw me come up to the floor and check in. It felt like a homecoming of sorts. My parents seemed relieved as well. There was so little to rejoice about during that solemn time, the smallest triumphs—eyes rolling back down in your head, a meal you could keep down, a private room on the "right" floor—were cause for celebration.

Spring had at last come to our corner of the world, and after a few days of steady rain, the grounds of the hospital were once again lush and green. From the window of the room, the garden below was beautiful and vibrant.

What made things even more incredible was a beautiful rainbow coming into the courtyard outside my window. It was one of the most beautiful things I had ever seen. I felt in my heart that I was warm, comforted, and that this was where I was supposed to be. The creation seemed personal, as if it had been cosmically brewed for me. It had to be a sign, a special message: a warning in my darkest hour that things would turn around. With tears in my eyes, I looked at my mom and said, "Everything's going to be all right, isn't it?"

She looked at me, and I think we both believed it when she said, "Yes, Sean, it is. It really is."

Aside from the hospital visits, I was also in and out of school. Once the chemo regimen started in earnest, it became impossible to keep up with work. The bad days were spent hunched over a toilet or getting ready to be hunched over a toilet. The "good" days were spent recuperating from being hunched over a toilet.

My attention span wasn't great on a good day; now it was short-circuited by worry and fear, doubt and uncertainty. Try concentrating on algebra or *The Canterbury Tales* when you've just gotten back from regurgitating the lining of your stomach or are waiting for your eyes to roll back in your head. "Impossible" doesn't actually describe the makeup work that was starting to stack up; "insurmountable" is more like it.

When I ventured back to school, I started wearing the wig Mom and Dad bought for me. Even though it was the best wig we could find—pre-Internet, of course; today I could find thousands of wigs to choose from, but back then not so many—it still looked like it belonged on the head of a middle-aged man, preferably one from the 1970s.

Naturally, I got tons of strange looks, and a few people asked me, "Sean, is that a wig?" Regretfully, I had to say yes, because the sideburns didn't look like they were attached to my head, and you couldn't see where the hair came out of my skin.

Regardless of how ridiculous it looked or what others might think, it was a comforting thing for me, my way of escaping what I was going through. Even though I knew it looked like a wig, it was one way of trying to be normal, and it protected me from everyone who was staring at me, everyone who looked at me like I didn't belong. It's strange what we grab on to in times of struggle or duress. That discount, polyester roadkill wig was my security blanket, a last grasp at normalcy when all around me swirled things I couldn't control.

A couple of times I tried to stay in school for the whole day. I probably forced myself to stay longer than was good for me. At first I could handle only about three and a half hours at a time, or half of an average school day. It was horribly draining on me—the hustle and bustle between classes, the long walk from chemistry class to algebra, the effort to put on a brave face when all I wanted to do was crumple into bed—and I would get incredibly run-down. Every day, however, I tried to go longer and longer and stay in school more and more. Unfortunately, one day my family received a call from the teachers to say that I shouldn't go to school because "so many people were sick" and I "shouldn't take any chances." I was told by my teachers that my parents should keep me home the rest of the week. Imagine that. Every teenager's dream scenario, right?

For me it was all about rest. I could turn off the alarm for the rest of the week and sleep in, catching up on my rest and trying to heal my battered body. We got about six inches of snow, and it was really icy, so there was nothing to do but sleep, eat, and sleep some more.

Around this time I had declared a moratorium on bathing, and as one might imagine, when the hormonal secretions of an average teen meet the absence of bathing, only one thing can result: stank. Mom and Dad finally talked me into taking a shower. I resisted at first, but in the end, good sense won out over bad smell. I decided that the hair was coming out regardless of what I was doing. If I showered, the hair was going; if I didn't shower, the hair was still going. So what did it matter? I should be clean, and I probably shouldn't stink or offend anyone around me; that was the least I could do, for all my family was putting up with. So I reluctantly hopped in and showered after a few days of being dirty.

My only real concern was that people didn't understand why I looked the way I did. At heart, I suppose I wanted my health crisis to stand for something. I wanted, more than anything, not acceptance or even respect but understanding. It bothered me that people didn't understand why this young boy was overweight, bald, and pale. Why he missed school so often and wore ill-fitting clothes and an odd-looking wig and was no longer the boy they used to know; not on the outside, anyway. Not to mention the sunken eyes, the constant look of exhaustion, and the aura of being . . . *ill*.

One day my dad overheard me lamenting the fact that my classmates didn't understand the physical effects of chemotherapy. He had a shirt made for me so people could understand my situation a little better. On the front, the green shirt said in white lettering, I DON'T ALWAYS LOOK LIKE THIS, while on the back it said pretty blatantly and to the point, so people would understand, I'M

ON CHEMO. (In the word "look," the two O's looked like eyeballs glancing to the right.)

Believe it or not, from time to time the chemo had its upside. Case in point: getting my braces off early. Before I was diagnosed with Hodgkin's, I had braces put on. So on top of everything else—the sideburn wig, the puffy face, the outgrown clothes, the sunken eyes—I was also a "brace face" or, during the holidays, "tinsel teeth," with dental rubber bands attached to the upper and lower jaws. Because I was going to be vomiting all too often, my orthodontist didn't think it was such a great idea to chance all the stomach acid getting behind my brackets and bands of the braces and, as he so delicately put it, "rotting my teeth away." So I was lucky I didn't have to wear them for too long, but I do still have a couple of crooked teeth. (It was a real shame, too, because I was just getting the hang of shooting those little rubber bands off my braces and hitting anyone I was aiming for.)

The entire time I was going through diagnosis and treatments, I felt like God had put my life on hold for a while. I joked around about Him "having the big remote control for life." The way I saw it, He had changed channels on me, surfing around for a while until He found the channel that I was supposed to be watching. It put a whole new emphasis on life. You never know when the channel might change, when things might go downhill, when you might get sick, so these days I always try to enjoy what I'm "watching" while I can. You never know when something might not go well, so go out and enjoy it now. That way, if something does happen, you can be glad that you didn't wait around to do what you should have done, like hold your kids for no reason, or play hooky to see that new movie you've been waiting for, or have a picnic with your best friend. If you want to do something and you have a goal, do it, don't wait, because your channel might change sometime soon—and quite unexpectedly.

I always thought it would be great if I could fast-forward through some (most? all?) of the crappy times and press pause or slow things down to enjoy the good times just a little bit longer. Watching my brother at a swim meet while I was sick, I was jealous that he was able to compete. I wished I could have worked harder, done more. Had I known what was going to happen to me, I would have done it differently. It's too late, and I can't go back to change things, so now I'm not taking anything for granted and am living every day to the fullest. Squeezing as much out of life as possible.

These weren't the thoughts of a teenager. These weren't things most kids thought about, but when you face your mortality every time you go back to the hospital, your wiring changes, pretty much forever. Suddenly, I was thirteen going on forty, and I knew more about life than most people my age could ever imagine. Usually, it was only my family and me, maybe Dr. Davis and a favorite nurse or two, who understood the full gravity—the serious danger—I was in because of this rare and deadly disease.

Other times the outside world came barging in in the most surprising and unwelcome ways. Because the prognosis was never very good and, frankly, was never in my favor, I was approached by the Make-A-Wish Foundation. Believe it or not, I told them to give the wish to someone else. The way I saw it, I was going to live and shouldn't take the gift of someone else who might not. My gift was giving that wish to someone else, not taking it for myself.

When I was feeling good (i.e., whenever I wasn't hunched over a toilet vomiting my guts out), I tried to keep my food down:

---

all of it, as much as possible, for as long as possible. I did the best I could and actually did a decent job of "eating my heart out." I ate as much as humanly possible because I didn't know how long I would keep things down and instinctively understood that my body needed more than I could possibly give it. In the plus and minus column of my digestive process, I was always operating in the negative. Therefore, I took incredible advantage of the days I felt well.

The doctors put me on an all-you-can-eat diet, so a regular breakfast morphed into as much as I could stomach. It was fantastic to be able to eat everything I wanted and as much as I wanted, too. A "normal" breakfast on this diet consisted of a few waffles with a powder protein mix in the batter, a two-egg omelet with cheese and meat, a can of roast beef hash, a muffin, three pieces of toast, a grapefruit, an apple, three to four glasses of juice, Canadian bacon, tea, cream of wheat, and whatever was on the table and popped up on my stomach's radar screen. Whew! When I wasn't vomiting, I was starving and ate like a garbage disposal.

Because I was eating so much, and because of the medicine, I got to be roughly sixty pounds overweight and incredibly bloated. I also wasn't having regular bowel movements and was always, as we liked to say in my house at the time, "clogged up." Going through chemo, your body becomes a specimen, and nothing is sacred. Everything is discussed—by everybody, all the time—to keep everything regular and in balance. It's hard at first, but it's like farting in front of a new girlfriend. For the longest time, you're incredibly uncomfortable doing it, but once it sneaks out, why stop? I was embarrassed about being clogged up for the longest time, but it was part of the treatment, and I shouldn't have been so concerned about it, because it was all for the greater good—my life.

Time and time again, events made me realize that there's so much more to life than what most people think (or what I thought before my diagnosis). Everyone complains about tiny things; they forget that they're lucky to be out of their house doing something and not running to the bathroom puking all over themselves. When a good day is making it to the toilet in time to heave up your entire digestive system, it makes you appreciate the before and after. I certainly don't wish the experience on anyone, but if I could bottle the feeling and sell it, I'd call it Appreciation Potion.

After I got myself collected and my bodily movements under control, a few friends started to come over. They were as unsure about the visits as I was, but then more started to come. It took a while, but I became comfortable enough not to wear my wig in front of them. It sounds like something small and minor, but I can tell you, back then that was a huge step for me.

Sometimes when I was feeling good, my family would try to get together and do something to get me out of the house. One outing in particular didn't turn out to be such a great idea, but at the time it seemed fantastic.

We ended up staying in a hotel in Sandusky, Ohio, a town about forty-five minutes away, for a little vacation. It was a good time for all of us; we were out of the house, away from the tug and grind of chemo and therapy and hospitals and doctors. All went as planned, though a few days after we got back home I told my parents I thought I was getting sick. I went to bed with a 99.5-degree temperature. Around one-thirty in the morning, I got up, started coughing, went to the bathroom, and Mom came in. She took my temperature again, and it was up to 101. She put a cold compress on my forehead to cool me off. Later, I took my own temperature, and it was even higher. We called the local doctor in Willard, and he told us to go to the hospital immediately and get some blood drawn to see what my counts were. If they weren't that high, he explained, I could take a prescription antibiotic orally. If they were high, I'd have to be admitted and started on an IV. Later that night, my dad made a land-speed record from Willard to Columbus as I passed in and out of consciousness because my counts were high and I had to be admitted into the hospital as quickly as possible.

By the time I was admitted, my temperature was over 105. They took some blood to see what was in the culture, but that apparently took a couple of days to grow. Meanwhile, my temperature went up some more. By the time the results were in, it turned out the cultures showed nothing. The doctors were scared it was pneumonia. After I'd spent five days fading in and out of consciousness, the fever broke and I was allowed to go home again.

While I was going through the treatments, my life was being bounced around, and my attitude was going through constant changes because of the hormones flowing through my body as a result of becoming a teenager. Like most kids, I would mouth off to Mom and Dad once in a while, but I'd also try to control it. For the most part, I kept myself in check and respected my parents.

My brother did his best to understand what I was going through, and I still feel sorry for what I put him through. I was temperamental and moody but did the best I could to keep my emotions from boiling over and to think of the other people around me first. Toward the end of that spring, I was going to school again and making it through every period except the first and last of the day. I even did some soccer practices after school. Running around like I used to and enjoying the fact that I could do something meant a lot to me. Now, don't get me wrong—there's no way I was running like I used to, but I loved being out there and at least *trying* to do something active. It was fantastic being outside and enjoying the weather, the sun, and the people I wanted to be with again—my friends.

A couple of times, during some games, I had the only allowable hand ball. My Hickman catheter protruded from my chest, and I could use my hands to protect it whenever the ball flew up toward me. My brother was on the sidelines for most of my games, cheering me on, as always. He's three years younger than I am and was never in the same league because they were divided up by ages. He was, however, always incredibly supportive and amazing at standing up for me.

One day he was on the sidelines during one of my games, and because every joint in my body was swollen, and I had perfect hair because it was a wig, some of the kids started poking fun of me and calling me Ken. I never knew about this until years later, when Seth broke down and told me, but it still makes me proud to know he stood up for me and told those kids to stop picking on me. He even tried to explain that the reason I looked the way I did was because I might die at any moment. Sad, I know; untrue, yes; but it sure worked! Those kids never picked on me again.

Eventually, I was able to play both offense and defense again, just like the old days. It was fun getting tossed around like I was one of the team again. I was having a great time—that is, until a head ball made me stop. The wig moved back on my head, and I ran to the sidelines and pulled myself out of the game. I was done. It also hurt so badly that I ended up getting a headache. My joints were swollen again, and I looked, like those kids had said, plastic.

While going through school and making it to the classes I could, I did the best I could on homework and quizzes and tests. A's, B's—I was doing fantastic for someone who wasn't in school for any great length of time in a row. I tried to do everything I could with the school and my friends, even the school dance. That's right, I went to the eighth-grade dance, and my friends rented a limo for us.

I was scared I wasn't going to make it all night at the dance, so Mom and Dad wrote a note letting the teachers know it was okay for me to come home early. It was fantastic. I had my first slow dance and hugged all the hottest girls "hello." Everyone was happy to see me, and I took full advantage of the benefits of the reunion. You see, after they all knew what I was going through, and they all understood why I looked the way I did, they accepted me. The teachers took it upon themselves to tell the students I had cancer and that they should all be nice to me because I might not live past eighth grade.

Okay, I'm not sure if they said that exactly, but the students did understand what I was going through and stopped pointing, stopped staring, and accepted me for who I was. I couldn't have asked for anything more.

I was feeling better about myself and starting to enjoy being alive. One thing that was never certain was if I was going to make it, because my emotions and thoughts were bouncing all over the place. There was always an underlying uncertainty about my life and about how my body was handling the treatments. However, when I look back at my mom's journal, I see a short excerpt in there quoting me when I was talking about my life and living and how much I appreciated it: "If I die, know that I had a really good life."

I couldn't have said it any better myself.

CHAPTER FIVE

A NOT-SO-NORMAL LIFE

❖

After months and months of intense treatment and my life slowing down to a crawl, I went in for another series of tests. I stopped counting the vials of blood the hospitals drew, or how many times I wrote my amount of pee on the wall chart, or how many other tests I had, some big and violent, some painless and small.

Some tests were simple, other tests left me weak and panting for days, and sometimes my blood count was too low and I couldn't take any of the treatments. My parents and I would hop in the car and drive ninety miles down to the hospital only to turn around and head home until my count got higher so my body could tolerate the treatments. Then it was right back to the hospital again. Looking back, I wonder how my parents did it.

When I hit my year anniversary, I had to go in for a series of hard-core, invasive tests to see how the cancer was doing. Was it still in my chest? Was it still all over my body? How were my lymph nodes? How was my body handling the treatments? So far, it had all been like one long bad dream. Now it was time to see if it would turn into a nightmare or I'd get to wake up and go free.

I realized at a very young age that health is precious, and too many people don't realize it until it's slipping away, or worse yet, it's gone. I didn't want to be like the adults I shared the ninth floor with, regretting their misspent youth, wasted time, or paths not taken. I'd hear them complaining to their spouses or children or the doctors or nurses that they weren't ready yet, that they still had so much left to do. I vowed never to be like that; either I was going to beat this thing and have the rest of my life to do the things I always wanted to do, or I was going to do them now, right now—come hell or high water—before this thing got the best of me.

I decided to live my life to the fullest. To live "Fearless," as I called it then, which is funny, because that was also the title of a short story I wrote during the course of my treatments for an Ohio Young Author's Conference and an assignment in English class. The story was about a young boy who was incredibly depressed and pondering suicide.

Near the end of the story, the main character walks up to the edge of a large, rocky cliff. With nothing to live for, the boy looks down to see where he is going to land: a rocky terrain void of any life, soon to be his final resting place. Getting ready to jump, the young boy takes a closer look and notices a yellow flower growing up and out of a crack in the rock. Improbably, this little flower has been strong enough to survive in a remote and hostile land, with no soil for nutrients, under the harshest conditions, in the fiercest of environments.

The young boy has two thoughts before he steps to the edge to plunge himself into the great unknown: The first is of hurting the flower, of not wanting to land on and kill the beautiful blossom as a result of this most selfish of acts. The second thought, and the one that has the most impact on our hero, is one of survival; of perseverance and resilience.

If this flower could live and survive by itself in the midst of some of the terrain's harshest rocks, and battle the raging elements on its own, then why couldn't the young boy? It is enough for him to rethink his life and realize that maybe he has hope after all, just like the little yellow flower. Maybe there is something deep inside him to keep him going, and quite possibly he can help someone else through some turbulent times by being an example.

I didn't win anything for the story, but it's something I still think about, and it makes me realize my profound thinking at such a young age. I had a lifetime of experience already. Was what I was going through teaching me something far beyond my years? Were there parallels between my own story and the boy I wrote about in "Fearless"?

Was I truly lucky?

Apparently so, because after I went into the hospital for the CAT scan to see if I was in remission (and after trying to get my mom and dad to drink the horrible barium milk shake along with me—with no success, I might add), the results came back negative.

I was confused for a minute—numb but confused, nonetheless: Wasn't negative a *bad* thing? So why were all the adults smiling? Then Dr. Davis explained that in this case, negative meant there were no signs of cancer in my lungs, not negative as in I wasn't in remission.

Positive. Negative. Up. Down. Didn't matter. That day I was given a clean bill of health. You would think that would be cause for celebration, and I suppose it was—for a few minutes, anyway. Unfortunately, that didn't mean the treatments would stop. Oh, no! All that meant was that I was going in the right direction and there were no *visible* signs of cancer in my X-rays and CAT scans. The treatments wouldn't end for a while yet; Dr. Davis had to assure himself that the rest of my body, the nooks and crannies hiding behind bone and lurking in the shadows left by the CAT scans or X-rays, were clean as well.

So if it wasn't exactly heaven, it was at least purgatory, a temporary reprieve. That meant I could start pushing myself again and trying to exercise more. It meant I could do teenage things, like grow and develop and flourish, and not hide like an old man with his wig on and bags under his eyes.

It also meant my psychological outlook was going to skyrocket. I could begin to think positively, without being afraid of jinxing myself. I might not have understood his terminology, but if there was one person in this world I could trust to tell me the straight dope, it was Dr. Davis. If he said my tests were negative, they were negative.

One downside of that day's tests was going from my "see food" diet (if I saw food, I ate it) to a strict, healthy, low-portion diet to lose weight again. Definitely not fun, especially if you've been given free rein of the kitchen for the past few months. I loved eating pizza whenever—and as often as—I wanted to. I loved taking advantage of that unlimited meal program; I felt like a bulimic in recovery. Now I was going back to portion control, which I hated, and exercise, which I loved. I was at least looking forward to the physical part, because I had always been active. I was especially anxious to get back into the water and try to swim again. But with my Hickman catheter still in my chest, I couldn't get into water any higher than my belly button. We didn't want to chance any infection. Kinda hard for a kid who was as much at home in the water as he was on land.

Also, because I was psychologically in the right state of mind and happy about being in remission, I was more open about my baldness and readily took off my wig in front of friends. It was so freeing to be able to let go of my security blanket, or barring that, at least to make fun of it from time to time. A few of us borrowed my dad's video camera one day and made a horror film called "The Attack of the Killer Wig." (Hysterical video; I wish I still had a copy.)

With the video, and the swim meets, and the short story, and the positive affirmations, I decided to make this cancer experience a positive one and use it for the rest of my life. In that sense, I was like a junior stockbroker; I wanted to spend money only if it was an investment. Likewise, I wanted to have only experiences that mattered, that counted, that taught me or somebody else a lesson. If life wasn't growth, if survival wasn't achievement, then what was I doing it for?

I suppose this experience made me a strong person, mentally and physically. One week ater a chemo treatment, I ran a 5K race. Not to win but to have a goal and to do something. To finish *something*. Granted, I didn't finish in any great time, but I did finish, and that was good enough for me. It was a goal I wanted to accomplish, and accomplish it I did. Think that made me feel good? Of course!

With school over, the summer swim season had officially started. Since I couldn't swim yet, I tried to help by coaching or doing whatever I could outside the pool. It's funny—ideas seem so good, deep inside your room, far away from the prying eyes of friends or family. I was given a clean bill of health, so the world was my oyster; unfortunately, the rest of the world doesn't always see it that way.

Case in point: Throughout all the summer swim leagues, I had never been beaten in any race and had numerous records to show for it. It was incredibly difficult going in the first few days and not getting in the pool, but what killed me even more was what the people on the team mumbled to themselves: "That boy looks like Sean. Even acts like him." It was as if they'd already written me off, as if I were already dead. Where did they think I'd been? Who did they think I was?

This was one reason to wear the "I'm going through chemo" shirt my dad had made me, so that people would understand what I was going through and know that it *was* me. Also, the coach told them why I looked as I did. When they realized it *was* Sean, they took me under their wings and understood what was going on.

Swimming is a very intimate sport. Unlike in other sports, where you are cloaked in shoulder pads and cleats and helmets, or covered up in jerseys and pants, you can't hide much in those tiny swim trunks. Your body is out in the open, out on display. The swimmers in the water were so robust and healthy; their development had played out as it should. Mine had been retarded, stunted; I was behind schedule, racing to catch up, figuratively and literally.

I felt more like a mascot than a participant, more like everybody's little brother than a competitor. But that didn't stop me. The same thing had happened in school, where I'd come from behind to catch up with my schoolwork and even attend the end-of-the-year dance. I looked at the pool as no different; I would have to work twice as hard, but that was no problem. I was happy for the work.

After all, it sure beat the alternative.

One day after coming home from the pool, I thought I should clean my room and start focusing on what was next in my life and getting over the cancer. Though I was still going through treatments, in my mind, I was done. I was no longer battling this disease, but taking the chemo to make sure, and only as a precaution.

It wasn't rash or foolhardy; it just was. I was done; I had won. The tests would confirm that, the doc was optimistic, my family was relieved, and I was tired of holding back and playing it soft. I was ready to run, jump, swim, play, fight back. I wanted a room that looked like everybody else's. I wanted posters of rock stars and celebrities and the Coors Light girl and athletes, like all my friends. I was making room for all the new trophies I'd win, the pennants of my favorite teams, the letter jackets and ribbons and citations and certificates.

So one day I decided to take down all the cards, letters of support, and banners. I spent all day rearranging my room and reflecting on all the support from family, friends, relatives, classmates, cheerleaders, even nurses and doctors and teachers. It was an end to my battle with Hodgkin's disease, chemo, and "what if" and "what for" questions.

I was packing away the frightening time in my life and putting away the wonderful support objects and special care I'd received over the past few months. Hopefully forever, except to take out later and reflect on those who helped me, who had faith in me and trusted that things would work out and I'd be in remission to begin my "normal" teen life again.

With things coming to a close, with my room back in order and my sickness neatly boxed up and put on a shelf, I wanted to support the swim team as much as I possibly could and try to set a new goal: to swim at the championship meet. Luckily, I was getting my Hickman catheter pulled less than twenty-four hours after my last treatment.

Doc Davis tried to make me feel better by telling me it wouldn't hurt one bit and that *he* wouldn't feel a thing. I wanted to tell him half jokingly, as he'd told me, "Um, yeah, thanks, buddy. *You* won't feel a thing, but what about *me*? Huh? The one here who's getting a tube ripped out of my chest? *You* won't feel a thing, but that doesn't make *me* feel any better."

Regardless, it was coming out, and I was ready for everything to be over, bad jokes and all. With one big breath, holding with as strong a grip as I'd ever seen, Dr. Davis pulled the flimsy tube out of my body, and for the first time in as long as I could remember, I no longer had a small snake protruding from my chest. I was no longer a cyborg but a normal kid. Okay, maybe a normal kid who was bald and a little overweight, but I knew I could take care of that. If I could beat cancer, I could easily beat being overweight.

Here is another illuminating passage from a journal my mom kept at the time, shared with me only years later, when she thought I could handle it. While reading it, I wondered how at times *she* had handled it, but as you'll see in this excerpt, my treatments and recovery truly were a joint effort:

Thurs 12:30 A.M. I can't understand how Sean comes up with the courage to have any more treatments, especially when he knows he's in complete remission. Brave—even more so than perhaps myself or many adults could be. He just doesn't complain—he endeavors it all without a question. He's so strong; perhaps this event in his life will make him a stronger person to face life and its trials. I never knew him to be so strong and courageous. "Learn life."

That's what I tell him. What a tough life to learn at an early developing age. Hopefully this will be life's toughest lesson for Sean to have to triumph over. An appreciation for life; Sean has a completely new outlook now. A whole new life lies ahead. This journal I dedicate to those afraid to try and fail. Sean, on the other hand, tried and tried and was a success. With lessons learned a few months ago yet untold to any of us.

Thank you, God, for this lesson with all the pain, suffering, hope, promise and joy you have unfolded. We can endure the difficult trials of this privilege you call life. You have opened our eyes that we may see. Your lessons have been embedded on our souls. We will try to thank you. We acted as a strong support system for Sean. It would vary what he'd want me to do when he started to get sick; he'd hit the wall and that noise through the intercom would wake me, but mostly I just lay awake waiting for the welcome noise from the intercom. He'd want the support and love, just knowing you were close.

At times he'd want me to help hold his hips steady as he leaned over the porcelain goddess throwing up his insides. A touch, a loving word. Just being there was the most Sean ever asked. Just three times do I ever remember him saying anything negative such as, "Why do I have to go through this?" or "I wish I'd not got sick." At those times I'd tell him, "You can do it. You have to be strong. It'll be over soon," but between you and me "soon" sometimes meant 36 or 48 hours. The love in Sean's eyes was more than enough. No "thank yous" were ever needed because I was there to see the end result, "live and in person."

Needless to say, after the last drip went through the Hickman catheter, I was ready to bolt out of there, but Mom and Dad wanted to hang around and thank Dr. Davis for all he had done. I can only imagine how emotional it was when they were looking into the eyes of the man responsible for saving their son's life. No longer was he Dr. Davis; he was Mel. We had earned the right to call him by his first name.

That summer was a breath of fresh air. Because I was helping with the swim team, I also had Dad drive me to another pool to practice on my own and get into shape for the championship meet. My goal was to make it up and back in the pool. It was an ambitious goal, to be sure, but not for a kid with all the time, energy, and motivation in the world.

I *really* wanted to beat some of the guys from the other teams, but come on, let's be realistic here. A kid who's still sixty pounds overweight and who just went through his last chemotherapy treatment, getting into shape and actually winning an event? This wasn't some after-school special, this was my life. The only competitive factor I had going for me was that I didn't have to wear a swim cap to cut down on the drag from having loads of hair, like everybody else on the team. I was bald! I had the best cap ever!

My mom suggested my goal should be K.I.S.S., or "Keep It Simple, Sean." So I followed her lead and kept it simple: Up and back, that was my simple goal. Some newspapers caught wind of what I was doing, and the *Mansfield News Journal* did a story on me. I was quoted as saying, "I want to show people that if you put your mind to something, you can do it. If you believe you can do it, go for it . . . you can do it." Pretty profound for a thirteen-year-old, huh? (The best part is that nearly twenty years later, my philosophy hasn't changed one iota.)

"You can do it." I did just that. I made it up and back in the meet. When it was all over, I got out of the pool and was drained;

every bit of energy I'd had was left behind in those chlorinated, churning waters. I also got beaten. I was no longer undefeated. However, I didn't care. Years ago I would have been crushed to see my old record fall; now I was elated to be getting out of the water in one piece.

The old rules had changed; new ones applied. I wasn't supposed to live longer than three months after diagnosis because my cancer was so advanced, and here I was, swimming in the summer swim league championship meet. I didn't care what anyone thought about me. I didn't care about anything but my goal and getting it done: proving to myself that I had it in me and I could do something.

Over the summer, I ran with the cross country team and managed to make some new friends, and by the time high school started, my hair was long enough that I didn't need a wig or a hat anymore. I was getting my body back into shape and enjoying everything I had been given again . . . my life! I was also incredibly lucky because I never got picked on. I was never hazed or put under the microscope or spotlight from the upperclassmen. I was the lucky one, and I knew it.

Did I take advantage of it?

You betcha!

Much as I hadn't been the typical cancer patient, I was far from the typical freshman. While my friends were meek and mild in the halls, minding their own business and getting to learn the ropes, I'd already learned them and was pulling on them as hard as I could. Pushing the upperclassmen as far as I could, trying to get a rise out of them—and everyone else, for that matter—was beginning to be a game for me. Luckily, I fit in with the cross country team really well and started hanging out with the upperclassmen right away. I had been through so much by this time, I realized there was no point in not trying to go after what I wanted.

Maybe it would work, maybe not, but either way, I was going to try and find out. I'd lost a lot of ground while I was sick and didn't want to waste another second of my youth on playing it safe. I didn't have time to ask for permission or wait for an invitation. I figured that I'd never know unless I asked, and the worst they could say would be no. So by the time Halloween came around, I had a girlfriend and was having a great time: hanging out with the juniors and seniors, running cross country, competing in track, and back in the pool. I was doing something every day and enjoying every minute.

All during my freshman year, I was also going in for my checkups for Hodgkin's disease. I started off going in once a month, then tapered down to once every three months. My parents, my little brother, even Dr. Davis, they were all so relieved, but none more so than I was.

Oh, sure, I'd hold my breath each time the doc came in to give us the good news—sitting on crossed fingers and staring down at my crossed ankles—but after a while, I got so used to hearing "negative," I forgot there could ever be such a thing as testing positive. The whole time, everything was smooth sailing.

When the summer swim season came around again, I was back in shape and ready to go. The weight was off, my hair was back, *I* was back. I was back to not getting beaten, and to setting more records than ever before. In a word, it was fantastic.

The only unfortunate thing was that in our team's thirteen-to-fourteen-year-old age group, we didn't have enough swimmers to have a relay. It takes four for a relay, and you can swim up in an age group, but not down. So when we were swimming against one of our longtime rivals, my friend Billy and I were used to swimming in the higher age group for the relays.

To make up for missing half of our relay team, Billy and I had this brilliant idea to swim the second-to-last relay exhibition (two events before the fifteen-to-eighteen relay). Exhibition meaning it wasn't points for the team, and we were doing it for fun. He swam first, I swam after he touched the wall, and while I was swimming, he was back up on the blocks ready to go in and swim again. While he was in the water, I was getting ready to swim anchor and the last two laps of the event.

Think it's exhausting to read? Just try swimming it. What we couldn't believe was that we were winning the entire thing by more than half a length. It was just the two of us against the other teams who had the requisite four people. We were having so much fun. Obviously, the other teams weren't too thrilled about the prospect of getting beaten by a team of two, and the coaches tried to disqualify us, but since we swam exhibition, they couldn't do anything.

We were always good winners, and never gloated, but inside, it was an awesome experience and a real triumph for both of us, me in particular. I wanted to dance around on the blocks and have such a good time, but I played it cool and tried to look the part as well. We ended up winning the next relay, too, but on that one, we had all four people.

Summer passed as quickly as our upstart relay; before I knew it, June was gone and July, too, and come August, it was already time for back-to-school shopping. Luckily, Mom and I didn't have to go anywhere near the Big and Tall section this year.

My freshman year had been a real triumph, and my sophomore year was pretty nice as well. I was continuing my check-ups every three months, and everything was going incredibly well there, too. I was still a little nervous when I went in for blood work, X-rays, and CAT scans, but every time I walked out of the hospital, I was in remission and a "normal" growing teen. This time the growing I was doing was up and not out. The weight was off, I was feeling incredible, had a stable of friends and my pick of girlfriends, was halfway through high school and on my way nowhere but up. I was doing well at school, with good grades, the girls loved me, the family was doing well, and everything seemed to be falling into place; I was walking on top of the world and enjoying everything I had been given.

There was no time to rest, not a moment to waste. The alternative was pushing up daisies, and that was not in my future. My job was to win, and there was no stopping me now. There was a song out at the time that I loved; they played it on every station, every hour. My favorite line was an appropriate one: "The future's so bright, I've got to wear shades."

That was me: young, pardoned, and facing a limitless future.

Who knew one afternoon in May, I would be sitting in the hospital, staring into an X-ray with a golf-ball-sized tumor attacking my right lung. It had all started to unravel a few days earlier. I'd been sitting in our living room watching TV, just like any other day. I don't really remember what was on at the time, because I was doubled over in pain, clutching my right side, with tears flowing down my cheeks, trying desperately not to fear the worst.

My family knew the monthly checkup was in a few days, so we decided to wait and not try to rebook my appointment. Somehow I made it. That day, that checkup, I'll never forget. I was peering into my X-ray, and the doc knew something was wrong, dead wrong. Later that day, I went in for a needle biopsy, and it was like déjà vu all over again: The practices and procedures were so familiar to me and my old team of nurses that we all could have done it by rote: They removed a lymph node, put in another Hickman catheter, performed a needle biopsy, put in a drainage tube, and started chemotherapy. Like clockwork, remission was over, and I was back in the thick of the C-word.

While we were waiting for the results of the needle biopsy (a delightful little procedure in which they took a nine-inch needle and slid it straight past my ribs to aspirate part of the tumor), I remember the doc talking to Mom and Dad. He was telling them that whether the cancer was benign or malignant, it had to be removed. So I was scheduled to get that taken care of as well. "The ninth floor," I wanted to joke but was in no mood to do so, "you're a one-stop cancer shop!"

In the operating room, I sat up on the table and asked for the surgeon. I was back to being cocky Sean, the high school sophomore with a new girlfriend for each weekend and life by the tail. Jokingly, I told him to make my scar look cool because, in the immortal words of the young and fearless, "chicks dig scars." I also remember mentioning something similarly pithy, like, "Oh, and don't forget to put everything back in when you're done."

Talk about creating Frankenstein: The surgeon had to slice about fourteen inches on my right side to get to the ribs, crack the ribs to get to the tumor, and for good measure, they removed a lymph node from the right side of my neck and placed a drainage tube in my lungs so I wouldn't drown in my own fluids.

Before I went in for the surgery, the doctors were telling me it was normally at least a two-week recovery in the hospital. I was shocked at this news and decided it wouldn't do for me. After all,

An allergic reaction caused my eyes to roll back into my head, and I thought I was going to lose my vision every single time. One of the scariest moments of my life.

At the age of thirteen, I had to inject myself with an anticoagulant so blood wouldn't collect in my Hickman catheter and kill me.

The second time through, I lost weight and just wasn't myself. I was walking around like a zombie.

Back in action and in the pool with a new head of hair growing back. I was on the road to being normal again. JIM JOHNSON/*MANSFIELD NEWS JOURNAL*

A lot of times, I wore my grandpa's old red one-piece while climbing. I looked like a fool, but it kept me warm until I actually got sponsorships and real clothing to wear in the mountains.

Waking up at all hours of the night and superearly in the morning isn't exactly conducive to being awake and ready to go all the time. Here I was getting out of "bed" for a hike up Grays and Torreys Peaks.

Sporting the new gear. Sponsors started helping out, and I had some decent clothing to wear in the mountains.

To get used to the frigid temperatures I was going to experience on Everest, I'd hike and climb around the Rockies in shorts, exposing my skin directly to the snow. Man, that was cold.

Whenever the sun was out in the mountains, I took great pleasure in basking in it and trying to soak up the warmth. Always with a smile on my face—snow, wind, sun, didn't matter. I loved life.

Grays and Torreys Peaks. Seth fell down the face of Torreys, on the right. Thought I was going to lose my brother forever.

On top of most 14-ers, there is a brass emblem from the U.S. government giving the altitude of the peak. This was from one mountain I used to run up—Bierstadt.

Here's what an Everest climbing permit looks like. My name is on the bottom right.

The Bhaktapur Cancer Care Center doctors and staff were more than happy to have us visit. I just hope I can get back there sometime to help with some support.

Seth hanging out with a yak on our way to Base Camp. It was incredible having my brother there to support me through everything.

From what I've been told, the highest pool table in the world.

Many of the bridges over the rivers we had to cross to get to Base Camp looked like this. Not very comforting to think the first Everest expedition ever probably went over this same one!

Home sweet home at 17,600 feet. For about a month and a half, pretty much every day started in snow.

Nima Gombu in the Khumbu Icefall where ice chunks the size of skyscrapers fall without notice and destroy everything in their path. Luckily we made it through safe and sound every time.

One of the many ladders we had to cross over crevasses. Metal crampons on an aluminum ladder aren't like Velcro. They're slick.

The Western Cwm was a huge bowl of ice and snow with temperatures sometimes reaching 115° F. Nima Gombu and I were relaxing for a bit before trudging the extra five miles to Camp 2.

Standing at about 21,000 feet holding the CancerClimber flag with names of people touched by cancer. In the background Lhotse and the Lhotse Face. Halfway up is Camp 3.

Stepping over a crevasse in the Western Cwm.

In the "Death Zone" at 26,300 feet, Camp 4 is nestled in the South Col. Tibet in the distance; Everest to the right.

The traffic jam that was the Summit Ridge after the South Summit (in the distance) and in front of the Hillary Step.

The Hillary Step was the last difficult section of the climb. A little up, a little to the left, around a huge rock, up a chute, and off to the summit in the near distance! Almost there!

May 16, 2002, 9:32 in the morning—the Summit of Mt. Everest. I'm holding a card that was blessed and given to me by Lama Geshi.

The very top of the world with the flag in the middle. The top of the world was dedicated to everyone ever touched by cancer.

Obviously I don't always look like this—two days postsummit. The sun's radiation gave me quite a burn, and I needed a haircut, but you can't fake that smile and those feelings.

One happy family. Seth, Dad, Mom, and me in the Denver Airport back home safe and sound. Now if we can just survive Dad's driving back to the hotel.

my track team had the Northern Ohio League Conference championship meet in under two weeks. A little thing like a golf-ball-sized tumor wasn't going to stop me from competing in that. My goal, as incredible as it seemed, was to make it to that meet and cheer on my friends and teammates.

When I woke up in the recovery room after the countless-hour surgery, my mouth was parched. Ice sounded so incredibly good, that was all I wanted. The only problem was that my brain, still under the influence of all the drugs for the surgery, couldn't put together that simple three-letter word. I-C-E. How hard is that to remember?

A nurse came by and asked if I needed anything. I told her yes, and she waited patiently for me to elaborate, but after sitting and thinking for about ten seconds, I couldn't come up with anything, and with a condescending smile, she said she'd be back. True to her word, she came back later and asked me the same question. My answer was the same. Ugh, I couldn't remember that easy little word, "ice." All I wanted—and all my mouth and body craved—was ice. Finally, she came around for the fourth or fifth time, and I still couldn't formulate the complex word, but out of my mouth popped the more complex "frozen water." She understood what I meant, and it was simple after that, but ice—I mean, come on.

Little did I know my release from the hospital was going to be as complex and unpredictable as getting ice chips after my surgery. Before I could win my freedom, I had to use an accordion-looking breathing apparatus and get to a certain level. It was a cylindrical object that sat on the rolling table where my meals were put so I could eat in bed. Inside the blue plastic frame was a clear plastic sealed container that was connected to a tube coming out of the top. It looked like something out of a sci-fi movie and was about as fun. Whenever I'd suck air out of the tube, the bottom of the accordion would rise up, and my air-intake measurement could be taken.

True to form, Dr. Davis was taking no prisoners; he placed an impossibly high mark on the machine and said if I got it to that level, I could leave the hospital. In his mind, he was thinking it would take me the expected two weeks to get there, but I think we'd been apart for too long, because he'd obviously forgotten the way I did things.

Through some of the most intense pain I have ever experienced, I tried to get the mark. Because I'd had my ribs cracked, every breath felt like the jagged bones were going to poke out of my skin, and the staples holding my hide together from the surgery were going to pop out.

Coughing seemed impossible, but to keep fluid from draining into my lungs, it became a painful necessity, and I learned over time to try to ignore pain in general, and doctor-approved torture in particular. I had a goal in mind, a singular, unrealistic goal, and nothing—not some machine from the future, not some deranged doctor, not some bone-rattling, bloodcurdling, skin-whitening pain—would stop me from making that track meet.

Fighting the pain, the tears, the racking coughs, the cracked ribs, the time line I had against me and that track meet, six days later, I was down at the hospital door, getting into the car with my dad to go to the track meet. That's right: I managed to get to the doctor's level (which would take at least two weeks for a mere mortal) in six days.

Dad took me to the meet and helped me into and out of the car. I couldn't use any of my back muscles, and every movement sent shocks to my brain, hitting every nerve ending and pain receptacle along the way. Regardless, I was there to watch and cheer on the team. News spread quickly to my teammates, who'd thought I'd be missing for at least the rest of the month. At the end of the meet, Willard ended up winning by a mere quarter of a point. It was incredible to witness, and at the end-of-the-year banquet, the team presented me with an engraved plaque: SEAN SWARNER, WHOSE EFFORT IS AN INSPIRATION TO US ALL. That wasn't my only gift; they ended up dedicating that quarter of a point and the entire meet to me as well. I was flattered, to say the least, and brought to tears.

In the meantime, the doctors back at the hospital—I was later to learn it was a whole team of them this time—were trying to diagnose what I was going through so they could begin treatment. My oncologist had never seen anything like it and made countless calls and spent endless hours of research trying to discover what had attacked my lung out of nowhere and so viciously. Maybe it was related to the Hodgkin's. Maybe it was a residual effect from the treatment and the chemo. Maybe we could have it explained.

Then again, maybe not. I was diagnosed with an incredibly vicious type of cancer (completely unrelated to Hodgkin's) that had, roughly speaking, a 6 percent survival rate. That statistic was far less sobering than this one: Out of every hundred people who got this type of cancer, ninety-four died. I've been told that I'm the only person in history—ever, anywhere—to have ever had both Hodgkin's disease *and* Askin's sarcoma. Not exactly the kind of world record I'd hoped to accomplish someday. If you're keeping score or have a copy of *Gray's Anatomy* handy, Askin's sarcoma is a type of Ewing's sarcoma but with a much lower prognosis.

I'll never forget the day I was in the hospital and we were getting the results of what exactly cancer type I had (this time). Dr. Davis asked Mom and Dad to step out into the hallway so he could talk to them in private. I knew what that meant, but this type of thing was old hat to me by now, and there was no way the grown-ups were getting anything by this vet of the ninth floor.

Being the sneaky teen I was, I grabbed my little buddy (otherwise known as the IV pole) and went to the door to eavesdrop. I wish I hadn't. The next few moments will haunt me for the rest of my life. It was simple and direct. Right to the point.

Mom asked him, "Is it cancer again?"

Doc simply replied, "I'm sorry, yes, it is."

Hearing this news brought me instantly to the edge of tears. I rapidly walked back to the bed to bury my face in the pillow. I'd gone through it once. I sure as hell didn't want to go through it again, let alone with the prognosis of a fourteen-day expectancy. That's right: I wasn't expected to live for longer than two weeks.

14 days.

336 hours.

20,160 minutes.

Sounds like a lifetime when you put it that way.

And it was; that was the lifetime they gave me.

Here I was on the cusp of my teen-hellion years, and my life was going in all the right directions—until this. I was at the top but instantly brought back down in a crashing way. The verdict, the death sentence, destroyed my inner self and everything I had been working on.

All of the philosophies, the platitudes, the positive spin I'd been putting on life, the universe, and everything: all gone. Even at my tender age, I knew lightning didn't strike twice, that I couldn't possibly beat the odds—and such incredible odds—a second time. Surviving cancer the first time was a miracle. Surviving it a second time? I didn't know what to call that.

It didn't really matter, though.

Somehow I knew I wouldn't be around long enough to find out.

CHAPTER SIX

FOURTEEN DAYS

❖

And so began the regimen of treatments—again. I couldn't believe it. After all my free days, all my positive affirmations, all my teenage confidence about insurmountable odds and how I'd overcome them, I was back to being the cyborg. The Teenage Mutant Ninja Tin Man connected to the tubes, wires, beeps, machines, and that stupid bed controller with the nonworking nurse button. The one I sometimes pushed over and over again, kind of like a game, just to see how long it took the nurses ("This is a test, this is only a test") to get there. That was around the same time I heard the wolf-in-sheep's-clothing speech for about the hundredth time. "All right, already," I wanted to scream, "I get it, I get it. Don't cry out for help when you don't need it."

It all came about innocently enough, or so I thought. One day I was playing around with the button, testing the nurses (for their own good, of course). I was also connected to the heart monitor. All of a sudden the monitor stopped the regular sixty-beats-a-minute blip I was used to and went to, drumroll, please, a flat line. A constant, solid beep. I had heard about this and seen it on TV over and over again, you know, the scene in the soap opera when the cast sits by the beloved star's bed as tears flow and that solid line keeps on sailing past the screen until, fade out, the soap star gets to try his hand at the big screen for a change, but this time it wasn't happening to Rick Springfield or Jack Wagner, it was happening to me.

I was dying.

My heart had stopped.

I didn't know what to do. *That stupid button,* I thought. I'd finally worn it out. I pushed it over and over again, and nothing happened. No one came until a little later. The entire time I could see on the monitor that my heart wasn't working, and I was completely scared out of my mind. Everything was going white, my chest was tightening, it was all over, I knew you were supposed to go toward the light, but there wasn't any light, and even if there was, I wasn't going to make it that far. I was dying. I felt like that old guy on *Sanford and Son:* "This is it! This is the big one! I'm coming to join you, honey!"

Finally, the nurses came in and saw that my heart (my heart!) wasn't working. I watched them coolly, calmly, a man enjoying his last few breaths, and noticed they were taking their time about it. As if they were doing a routine maintenance check, they ever so casually walked over to the machine, followed the cord back to where it was connected to my body (it was supposed to be on my finger at the time), and there it was—dangling from the bedside railings.

I wasn't dead after all.

The stupid finger/pulse/heart monitor thingamajig had fallen off and couldn't detect a signal. After that I no longer played with the nurses' button to time how long it took them to get into the room (although secretly, I felt they suffered from the lack of practice). I just played with the bed buttons instead and saw how fast I could surf through the TV channels. To this day I can still zip along and see what's on each channel in a fraction of a second. I became the remote-TV-surfing master.

Those were the fond memories, the intermissions, the brief reprieves in the otherwise grim litany of my second diagnosis. This time around, the treatments were worse, *much* worse, and my family and I were warned well in advance that they would be incredibly hard on my body. So hard they were divided into two treatments (just like the Hodgkin's), but each time I got a chemical cocktail, I was admitted into the hospital and made unconscious.

That's how bad my own personal cancer sequel was: I was in a medical-induced coma when I was receiving the chemo treatments. I'd go in like the first time, for a weekend, off for a week, back in for a week. That was where the similarities ended.

My body was so weak, my appetite so small, that this time I lost sixty pounds. I was downright unrecognizable. It wasn't just "poor Sean, look how thin he is," it was more "Sean, is that really you?" I might as well have been from a third-world country, suffering from diphtheria and carrying around my UNICEF box on Halloween, asking for donations.

The first three months were so intense, my hair pretty much vanished instantly. Just like that. One day it was there; the next time I had the strength to feel my head or got around to looking in a mirror, it was already gone. Oh well, at least I didn't have to agonize over choosing a wig or avoiding the showers this time around.

The doctors wanted to put me in that coma so I wouldn't remember anything I was going through. It worked, for the most part. But I do remember the good times, and though there weren't very many, I lived for those.

Case in point: Thanks to the rapid hair loss, I was the only kid in school allowed to wear a hat (when I was actually there). I know it's not much, but when something bad happens, you try to make the most out of the highlight reel. There was more cause for celebration—I'm also the only person in the state of Ohio who has ever had his driver's license taken with a hat on. The people at the local DMV let me take it like that, and I felt like the coolest person in the world. (My guess is that Mom or Dad made a few phone calls to make that one happen.) Anything large or small that I could look forward to, or that made me smile, and I was instantly on cloud nine.

This time I was more shaken up by the treatments and how they affected my appearance. I was in high school now, and more concerned about how I looked than ever. I didn't want to be a freak. I didn't want a wig. I didn't want to look different, but the fact remained, I *was* different. I did everything I could to fit in and not let people know I was bald. More than likely, I drew more attention to myself by wearing a hat in school than I would have if I was bald.

This time, or so I thought, I would be just a super-skinny kid and blend in with everyone else, but instead, I was in and out of the hospital so often that I wasn't enrolled in classes for a single term. I basically missed a year of high school. I was gone too much, and there was no possible way for me to keep up with all the work. When I was feeling better, we looked into enrolling me into one class for one grade, to keep me involved with my peers, my friends, and the school setting. Sounded good in principle, and it was something I was really looking forward to. Only one problem—the OHSAA and their rules.

The Ohio High School Athletic Association had this rule that even if you were enrolled in one class and didn't participate in any sports whatsoever, you'd still lose all of your eligibility for sports. Meaning, in two years, I wouldn't be able to participate in anything the last semester of my senior year in high school. What kind of crap is that?

Basically, a student was allowed eight terms of eligibility, and that was it. It didn't matter what you were doing, why you were doing it, or even if you were participating in any sports while you were doing whatever you were doing that they already didn't care about. All that mattered was that you were in class and present. Period.

In my eyes, that's not right. Someone could go (like me) to school for one class, just to be a part of the school process, to have friends, and to maintain some sort of social life while battling a disease, but be ineligible for his or her senior year of sports. Not right and completely unfair. So unfair that my dad personally went to the board of the OHSAA and pleaded my case. I'm not certain what happened in that room, but I know tears were shed, and while the board was voting, an incredibly arrogant and insensitive reporter came up to my dad and said, "You know you're dead, right? They never change rules."

I would have liked to see that reporter's face when he read the headline in the Cleveland *Plain Dealer* sports section the next day that said, SWARNER'S BREAKING RECORDS AND THE RULES. They voted six to one to overturn that rule. Another Ohio first! I could go to class and become a "normal kid" (too bad OHSAA couldn't wave their magic wand and put sixty pounds back on me; now, *that* would have been a real Ohio first), without worrying about being ineligible for sports in my senior year in high school. I don't think I could ever thank my dad enough for doing that. It gave me a new lease on life; I was given a second chance, and I knew things would be okay from that moment on. Just like the rainbow the first time with my mom, this was my sign of hope. And even if things weren't okay, I was going to have one hell of a time until it was all over.

Not all my timing was good that year. My radiation treatments started about the time when I was getting my permit to sit behind the wheel of our family car. Then again, maybe it *was* a good thing: I got in tons of practice, because I was supposed to get the radiation treatment once a day for five days in a row for an entire month. Every Monday, Tuesday, Wednesday, Thursday, and Friday, we hopped into the car to drive ninety miles each way to get the treatments. I believe they lasted about thirty minutes or less. Then it was ninety miles back home.

That meant every day, Monday through Friday, I got 180 miles of driving practice. Needless to say, and I'm going to toot my own horn here, I'm a good driver.

The radiation treatments weren't too bad, because they were localized on the upper right section of my chest. No chemo this month, because it was going to be all zapping in my chest, and no vomiting, either. No toxic cocktail for this boy, no sir, it was all invisible radiation being bombarded through my body to kill whatever may have been left over after they sliced it out of my chest during the operation (thoracotomy).

My hair was starting to grow back in, and by the end of the month, and the end of the radiation treatments, I wasn't wearing a hat anymore. That wasn't the only new development; I also had, drumroll, please, ta-da, a date. That's right, I had a date with someone, and because I had my license by this time, I could drive somewhere and not just watch a movie downstairs and make out.

We could have a conversation, talk, get to know each other, then make out!

Well, you might have guessed it: The hair—and the date—lasted about as long as this sentence. It was over before it began. The month passed, and the radiation treatments stopped. It would have been nice to say that was the end of the treatments, but this is no Hallmark story. Fact is, the treatments were only beginning.

According to my doctor, after the radiation treatments, I had over ten more months (not weeks, *months,* as in forty weeks) of chemotherapy to go. The cycles started again, and I missed the rest of the year. Just like that, my teen dream turned into a living nightmare. Gone were the days of driving and dates and hope and forever. Now I didn't know what day it was. I never knew what was going on and was in a complete fog most of the time, never sure what was happening with my body, even less sure about what was happening in my life.

Life? There was no life, only the hospital, the treatments, the cycles, the measurements, the comas, and the sad, unfiltered truth: I was sick, and only chemicals, the same kind of chemicals they use in bombs to kill people, could save me. Forget cyborgs and robots and beeps and buzzers, it was back to my own personal zombie movie, 24/7, for the next ten months (forty weeks).

More weight melted off (go past zombie straight to mummy, do not pass go), and I kept getting sicker and sicker. I did my best to keep up with school—I was auditing a class, because that was all I could handle. I wasn't going for a grade, but simply being in class with my peers was good enough to keep me going. Sad as it was, it helped me look forward to something as opposed to lying at home on the couch, or worse, in the hospital bed waiting for the next nurse to come in and suck out some more blood (zombies and mummies and vampires, oh my).

Believe it or not, when I was diagnosed with the Askin's sarcoma, my old pal Mel (that's Dr. Davis to you) didn't know what I had until he'd done a ton of research. He was asking colleagues, investigating the latest research, making phone calls, before he finally found out what I had. But that was only part of the process. He then had to devise the treatments to make me better again (oh yeah, and beat the crap out of this cancer as well).

Askin's is an incredibly rare tumor. So rare that someone in Texas actually sent us a card in the mail to say that a high school student there had Askin's as well, he'd been diagnosed with it a short while after my diagnosis. We corresponded for quite some time, a few cards, some goofy letters on notebook paper (hey, I had plenty left over from that year's back-to-school shopping). Basically, we became each other's fan club. Unfortunately, after several rounds of chemo, he didn't make it. It goes to show you that even with all the advanced medicine and machines and radiation and expert care, surviving cancer is still one big crap shoot.

Who knows why he died and I lived? My protocol must have been different, or maybe I was just plain luckier. I don't know. And to top it off, with the other cancer before Askin's my treatment was completely experimental. I must say I'm probably one of the luckiest people on the face of the earth.

In fact, the way normal checkups go after treatment is complete, people go in once a month to do blood work, X-rays, or whatever their doctor wants them to do. After a certain period of time, they go in once every three months, then six months, then a year. For whatever reason, my family and I were almost at the six-month mark and decided to do four and a half instead. As for me being lucky? Maybe that tumor wouldn't have shown up in the three-month checkup, but I'm pretty certain if we'd waited until the six-month one, I wouldn't be here right now.

Another thing that set me apart from a lot of the other kids going through cancer was that I read a few books about visualization. There weren't many at the time, but believe it or not, I experimented with them. I was up for anything by this time, and visualization seemed as good as anything else I'd heard about so far.

Every day I'd picture my cancer like this monster. (What else, right? Might as well stick with the running theme.) These horrible, disgusting monsters were invading my body, and the chemotherapy was like a futuristic cavalry attacking the monsters. They'd go in with their guns, ammo, knives, and tear apart the monster that was killing my body. Every time I got sick, every time I retched or emptied my stomach, I was getting rid of the bad cells in my body, puking up the monsters. Obviously, monsters couldn't live in stomach acid, and I had to get rid of them somehow after the cavalry dropped them in jail (my stomach).

Close to the end of the chemo treatments, I was getting tired of being sick, tired of the agonizingly slllooooowwwww drip . . . drip . . . drip of the medicine into my system. So sick of it that I tried to convince my doc to speed up the chemo drip so I could head out earlier to get to a home track meet and support my team. It must have been a Friday, since track meets were usually on Saturdays. Anyway, I pictured every drip . . . drip . . . drip as another troop of good guys going into my veins to kill the bad guys. Like the army or secret agents. I'd play around with it, because in my mind, the cancer monster got smart, so we'd have to sneak up on it sometimes. My heart was where the platoon gathered and was sent out to do its mission, kind of like cancer ground zero; I pictured them landing, parachutes filtering in through my bloodstream, army helmets and big guns on tripods, and sweaty soldiers prepared to do battle to the death.

I told Mel that I needed to get out of there; I had to be at the meet for my team. I wanted to cheer them on and would do anything for them. The doc saw in my eyes that I wasn't joking and knew my focus was intense. He was reluctant because he thought I'd be too tired from the treatments, but he agreed that it was okay for me to go and said that if I got the chemo done, I was good to go. Little did he know I would be heading out of that hospital very early the next morning and the family would be driving the familiar ninety miles back home to Willard to support the team.

Dr. Davis was astounded that my determination would take me to the meet sick, exhausted, etc. Obviously, he didn't subscribe to the same philosophy I did—that if you put your mind to something and have a never-say-die attitude, you can do anything. The whole way back home, I kept telling Dad to drive faster because I'd miss the meet. Mom and Dad weren't sure I should go because of how tired I was, but they knew I wanted to see my friends and become a "normal" kid again. Even if it was for only a few minutes.

We parked the car, and I saw all my teammates, friends, and coaches in their pre-meet huddle. I let them do their thing, but when it was over, I was surrounded by them all to wish me the best. I thought they had it all wrong—I was there to wish *them* good luck, not the other way around. They were incredibly shocked to see me, and my little brother, Seth, ran up to me and gave me a big hug hello. I think he was relieved to see his brother home again.

Looking back, I marvel at the audacity I had, and I wonder what went through Dr. Davis's mind as he watched me run these fool's errands. But so many incredible things had happened, so many things that shouldn't have happened, I think he gave up that day and resigned himself to the fact that this crazy kid was going to do it his way, and most times my way actually worked.

Be it visualization or track meets, zombies or mummies or vampires or cyborgs, I think I survived not in spite of being a rash, foolhardy kid but *because* I was a rash, foolhardy kid. We all live differently, we all die differently, so why shouldn't we survive differently as well?

My releases from the hospital would come at all hours of the night or day. It became a familiar routine for everyone in the family. Dad had to work, but he took off Wednesdays and was driving to Columbus every Tuesday night. Seth got shuffled off to one of our close family friends and stayed with them whenever both Mom and Dad were at the hospital with me. I still feel bad for dragging everyone through all this muck, and I wish I could have done something different for my brother, but he's incredibly supportive now, and I can't thank him enough. Then again, maybe he should be thanking me for enabling the sleepovers at his friends' houses on weeknights.

There was another kid, Danny was his name—the only other young guy on the ninth floor—who was about my age at the time. I remember he played football. (Funny, the things that stick out now.) He was diagnosed with a brain tumor and was my roommate at one time. That one time turned into many times, and we'd sit and talk while we waited for our poisonous cocktails to drip into our bodies. It's a very intimate experience, waiting to die. You get real close, real quick.

Danny had a younger sister, so my brother finally had someone to talk to about the whole ordeal, but unfortunately, neither of them chatted too much, since they were too worried about their respective brothers (God love 'em). It also gave my mom and dad some other people (Danny's parents) to talk to. At that time there was no such thing as a group session for cancer patients and their loved ones, so maybe this is what we all needed—someone, even one person, to talk to.

Danny and I became pretty good friends over the times we were in the hospital together. Every time I'd be admitted onto the ninth floor, I'd request to be his roommate so we could share our treatments and go down that horrible road side by side. It became almost like a ritual. Every time my family and I went to admitting, I'd ask, "Did Danny check in? If so, could I please have him as my roommate?"

I wonder sometimes what the nurses thought, seeing the light go on in my eyes, this new enthusiasm to be checking in. Did they know how it would all play out? Had they been down this road before? If they had, they weren't 'fessing up to either of us. (Thank God.)

We would talk together, eat together, watch cartoons together, throw up together. We even got into contests. My favorite was to see who could go home first. We'd watch the final drips from the IV bags go down the tubes into our Hickman catheters, and bam, "Ha ha. I get to ditch this place first! You poor bastard. See you next round!" We'd leave each other with smiles but tears in our eyes because the truth was, we never knew what would happen and whether we'd see each other again and, if so, in what condition. What type of health? Would I be better, or would he?

Then the day finally came. I went in and he wasn't there. No sign of him, and no one knew what had happened to him, when or where. I was lost. He didn't make it. He finally gave up after all the treatments. My best hospital friend was gone, and so was my hope—until I found out it was quite the contrary.

He was alive and over his cancer.

He was done with his illness and in remission.

He was one of the lucky ones.

He had made it. Would I?

CHAPTER SEVEN

THE COMEBACK

❖

Truth be told, after the OHSAA ruling and entering that one class for the winter/spring term, I really put my nose to the grindstone and tried to hammer out some good grades when I was feeling decent. Moving forward in fits and starts, I was like a bear hibernating. When I was finally able to "wake up," there was a blizzard of activity and so much life to catch up on. Because I had missed an entire year of school, I couldn't graduate with my class and got held back in the eleventh grade.

The teachers would let me get away with more than most of the other kids, and I surely took advantage of it. Roaming the common areas during study hall became my norm. I wonder now if any of the teachers ever noticed that my friends all seemed to ask for a hall pass at exactly the same time.

The locker room became our hangout while we were all supposedly out on extended hall passes. I'm not even sure how it happened, but one of my friends on the cross country team "found" a set of keys, and early in the morning, we'd come in to do a mile on the track, eat breakfast in the locker room, and test out the keys around the school. Some of them opened up offices, classrooms, and private areas that students weren't supposed to see, like the teacher's lounge. Let's just say we had some fun with those keys, and I think they're still floating around the school, in the possession of the cross country team. (Until one of my former coaches read this, that is.)

It may seem strange to picture me near death in the hospital bed one minute, and then slipping out of classes during study hall and hanging with the cross-country team, but such is the beauty, the miracle, the mystery of the teenage body. Downtime was dead time, lost forever and never to be regained, but when I was up, when I could eat and sleep without drugs and drive without puking, it sometimes seemed as if nothing had happened at all.

Such were the powers of recuperation that, at the time of my chemo treatments, I was actually running ten miles a day. Naturally, Dr. Davis told me that this wasn't advisable, but I honestly think it's one of the reasons I'm alive. I exercised even while I was sick and pushed myself to the limit when I felt good. I think it made my body handle the treatments better and recover more quickly. I didn't get as sick, and I had more energy.

February 2, 1991, was a date I will always remember: It was my first time back in the water at an official swim meet. Because I had my Hickman catheter pulled early, I was swimming with the team, trying to do as much as I could while still undergoing treatments. Since I had that "chemo snake" slithering out of my chest (although it probably would have looked right at home), I couldn't train that well for swimming. Okay, I was in pretty decent shape from the running, but there's a reason athletes pick one or two sports—and usually in the same field—in which to specialize: Switching up isn't as easy as it looks.

Even though I was bald from the medicine, I had been training with a cap on, because I was embarrassed about my looks. I was training with a YMCA swim team about thirty minutes from home. When I couldn't make it there, I drove to a closer facility to train by myself, because Willard didn't have an indoor pool where I could train.

After my trials and tribulations, every family on the Bucyrus swim team knew I was sick and trying to get back into shape, so when February 2, 1991, arrived and the official swim meet began and I got up on the blocks to swim the 100 freestyle, the natatorium was packed. Not just with friends, teachers, doctors, nurses, and classmates, either; it was a real family affair: Mom was officiating, Dad was in the stands, and good old Seth was standing faithfully on deck. Since it was the first heat of the event (they put the slower kids up first and the fastest ones in the last heat), I was swimming against just one other person. (He was an exchange student from Finland, I think.)

The buzzer blared and we both dove into the water. I kept up with him the entire time. Stroke for stroke, turn for turn. In a 100-meter event (if it's a short-course pool like the one I was competing in), you swim four laps: up, back, up, back. Each turn I was with him all the way; I felt incredible.

The last turn, I pushed off and saw him a little ahead of me. It was the ultimate motivator; this was my *Rocky* moment, and I'd be damned if I was going to let the champ beat me in the final round.

Though I was trying as hard as I could, pulling as hard as possible, I think the people in the stands could see the piano fall from the sky and land flat on my back. "The wall" was huge, brick, and reinforced with steel. I died. I went kapoot and couldn't find any strength at all; the steam was gone, and there was no more fuel for the fire. I felt horrible just trying to keep up, forget about passing him. I could no longer stay with him. I ate his wake and lost the race by about three seconds.

Yeah, not too shabby for someone who had cancer and was going through chemotherapy, but I wanted to win. Besides, I never wanted to win that "not too shabby for someone who has cancer" prize. The worst part was, I really thought I was going to win. Regardless, I finished. I made it, and when I was crawling out of the pool, the entire natatorium was echoing with thunderous applause. Everyone on deck, in the stands, and around the pool area was on their feet, giving me a standing ovation, cheering and clapping for about five solid minutes longer than it took to swim the race!). Taking my *Rocky* moment anyway, I put a towel over my head, sat down in the chair behind the block, and smiled to myself.

My first thought was not of disappointment, fatigue, failure, or dejection, but one of positive affirmation: "I did it—again."

Back into the hospital I went for some more treatments. Because I had my catheter pulled early, I had to get an IV from here on out, but it was worth it, because I could get back into the water and swim again. The good news was that because I was training, running, swimming, and lifting when I was up, I didn't get tired, like I usually did when I was down. Instead, I was bored. I was still upchucking and not feeling great (not something you ever get used to, by the way), but I did what I could and wasn't as sick as normal. Every time I'd go in, I'd have this game I'd play to annoy whoever was in the room—Mom, Dad, anyone who came to visit. I'd go up and down and up and down and up and down with the bed. The foot of the bed, the head of the bed. Finally, I think Mom got sick and tired of it because she unplugged the damn thing.

Nice going, Mom. Now I had to find something else to do to bother people.

So in and out I'd go for a few more months, until the last drip of chemo got into my system. By this time I had my mind made up that I wasn't going to get sick. Period. End of story. Didn't matter what the results said, or Dr. Davis, or Mom or Dad, or anyone; it just wasn't going to happen. Not this time; never again. As with the first time, I made the decision, and I understood deep in my soul that I wasn't going to vomit. I had done enough of that and was tired of it. Over. Never again. I was placed in remission and set free in May 1991.

To say this cancer was a walk in the park would be something of an understatement. To say I had some hardships would be the same. To say it was the hardest year in my life would be more appropriate. Within a year, I had been diagnosed with a cancer bearing a truly grim 6 percent prognosis. I was given two weeks to live, and I was approached by the hospital to make a will, encouraged to enter into hospice, and worst of all, at the age of fifteen I had my last rites read to me. By all means—and by all accounts—I should be dead. Without a doubt, I'm a living, breathing, walking miracle. Think about that for a minute. I had my last rites read to me by a man of the cloth. I was fifteen years old. Goes to show that the old saying "It ain't over until the fat lady sings" is the truth!

Summer came, school was over, and it was time for the summer swim league again. With a clean bill of health, I immediately got into that pool and started tearing it up, zipping up and back during practice and meets. I was back, and I was back in a powerful, lasting, significant way. This year I wasn't going to be beaten.

I had my eyes set on some more records and was like a dolphin in the water. Some of those records still stand because I was pushing my body past what I thought it could handle.

Each time I won a race, set a record, or shaved so much as a fraction of a second off of an existing time, tears were dripping down Mom's and Dad's faces, as well as those of the countless people around the pool. Knowing what I had just accomplished gave everyone on the team incredible motivation. An air of success swept over the pool each time I came out of the water.

I say this not as a way to inflate my own ego or dramatize my achievements, but to look back and reflect upon how involved everyone had become in my recovery. I had never been big on community before; we lived in a house on a street and shopped at the grocery store and went to the mall. Classmates were classmates and teachers taught and the postman delivered the mail, but going through all that I did, and watching so many people respond with generosity and sincerity, really made me feel like I was home, like I belonged in that pool, swimming those races for those cheering people; that each time I won an event, they remembered that life was precious, that miracles do happen, and that anyone—even an occasionally bratty, sometimes silly practical-joking fifteen-year-old who'd been on the threshold of the great hereafter and came back to kid about it—can beat the most incredible odds if they simply don't give up.

For me, the struggles went on, even if they were in a pool rather than a hospital room. If I was in pain, I would always compare that pain to the bone marrow test I endured when they were diagnosing me with my first cancer. I knew what pain was, and it was never going to reach an eleven on a scale of one to ten because of a leg cramp or side stitch. No way, no how.

As a result of this painless, fearless new philosophy, I managed to set a number of new records in swimming and had the attitude that I could take on the world. Not an arrogant, pompous attitude, but one of loving life, living each day to the fullest. When I won those races, I'd never taunt the other person or shove it in his face; I'd reach across the lane line and shake his hand and say, "Hey, man, good job." This may surprise you, but I have to admit that I did have some meets when I was a little arrogant, though it was always in good fun (at least on my end) and only with people I knew could take it.

Donny was my competition. His mom was the coach of another team, and he and I always bantered back and forth; "trash talking" is what they call it in other sports, but in the pool we call it "splash talking." One time he was diving (we did both diving and swimming), and the speaker shouted out the next dive attempt would be a "reverse three and a half, two twists."

Excuse me? Did I hear that right? Are you kidding me? I had to check this one out. Sure enough, he got up at the end of the board, did his approach, and the board sprang him high into the air. He sat there, suspended in midair like Air Jordan in a Speedo, as we waited, breathless, below. Next thing I knew, he was coming back into the pool, doing a cannonball. A cannonball, of all things! *Fantastic*, I thought. Funniest thing I'd seen in a while. But that was the kind of kid Donny was: a kindred spirit, I guess you could say.

Naturally, behind the blocks, we'd go back and forth, pushing each other, picking on each other, the typical good-natured, competitive stuff kids do every day.

"Think you'll keep up this time?" I'd taunt.

"What you got?" he'd come back and say to me. "You got

nothing!" After it was all said and done and I touched the wall first, we were still friends, and we always had smiles on our faces because we were having a great time. Great time? Another understatement; I was having a fantastic time. It was the summer I had always wanted, always dreamed of, during those long, endless nights leaning over the porcelain god or watching my hair fall out or checking in on the ninth floor.

I could drive, I was free, and I was alive. Talk about an endless summer.

Conference champs came to an end for the '91 swim season. I'd set a few records along the way, but what hit me the most was when my brother broke one of my records. Ouch. Yeah, that hurt. I'd worked so hard to get that set when I was younger, but he broke it in the 50 breaststroke. Eventually, he was better than I was at swimming, and if someone had to break my records, I wanted it to stay in the family and be my brother. After all, I'd much rather have him break it than someone I didn't even know. (Good job, Seth!)

School started up again. It felt like my senior year, but officially, I was a junior. After swimming, I was running with the cross country team again, trying to get—and stay—in shape. Even though I wasn't as successful in my track and field career as I was in the pool, I was out there and enjoying everything with all my friends. I couldn't help but be addicted to running. It was so freeing, so positive, so good for the soul. Every mile I ran felt like it took me one step farther from the disease, as if I could outrun death itself.

I suppose I wasn't the only one to try and cheat death: Shane (one of my best friends) bought a motorcycle during this period and loved riding around. Like me, he had a flair for life and loved adventure.

This was the year I was supposed to graduate—1992—however, since I missed a year, my year would be 1993. No biggie; I'd made it this far, and I wasn't going to let pushing back graduation by a year stop me now.

Later that year, my family took a skiing vacation in Colorado. We had a fantastic time out there, shooshing in the powder, zipping in and out of the trees, and jumping over every little bump we could find. For me, it was more confirmation that being physically active and challenging the elements yielded cathartic experience. The trip was once-in-a-lifetime for us, especially after what we'd all been through.

Coming back home was a different story.

I remember it like it was yesterday. I was sitting in our family's living room, watching the local station that has hometown news on it, updates for school closings, the menu for the next week of school, "the boring one," as Seth and I called it back then.

I was sitting in the chair. The same chair I was sitting in when I felt the pain in my side, three days before I was diagnosed with Askin's. Then something flashed up on the TV. I wasn't sure what it was at first and wasn't quite sure I'd read it right: "Donations for the Shane A. Parsons Memorial Fund will be accepted . . ."

I was in disbelief. I waited until the cycle of news came around again to make sure I had read it right. Mom, Dad, and Seth were all doing something else, what, I don't know. I didn't care. I sat in the chair through three cycles of the news until the phone rang. The sound didn't surprise me; I suppose I'd been waiting for it to ring.

"Sean, it's for you," my mom said. I picked it up, and on the other end was another good friend of mine: Without even saying hello, he said, "Sean, did you hear the news about Shane?" I lost it. I couldn't control myself and started bawling my eyes out. Shane, one of my best friends, had been killed while riding his motorcycle. His new motorcycle. Apparently, he was passing a semi, and without signaling, the semi turned sharply left and Shane smacked into the side of it. He died instantly, on impact: No chemo or catheter could save Shane now.

To this day, whenever I do something I know he'd like, I look up to the sky and wink, knowing he'd love to be doing it with me. Like when I went bungee jumping, sky diving, surfing, or even when I had a motorcycle myself. Every time I got on the motorcycle, I thought of him and never did anything stupid. He's been my guardian angel.

Bungee jumping—I knew he'd like to do that, but on the funny side of things, Dad videotaped me jumping out of the crane. It was okay with him but not okay with Mom. If you listen closely on the video, you can hear my mom in the background, saying, "Scott, if that bungee cord breaks, our marriage is over!"

The graduating class of 1992 was my "real" class: my friends, the people I had known for just about twelve years. I grew up with those people. I carpooled with them in kindergarten. I got kicked out of the front seat because I never let anyone else ride up there when we were on our way to school. We all knew one another incredibly well, and we were close. It hurt knowing they were leaving for bigger, better things and I was staying behind, stuck with the same old Tater Tots in the cafeteria and announcements over the intercom.

I wanted to be a part of this somehow, and my wish came true when I was asked to escort the entire class down the aisle during graduation and congratulate each and every one of them after they got their diploma onstage: I was kind of like an honorary principal, minus the big blue sash. It was an incredible honor, and I was happy I could be there for them and thank them for being there for me. Again, I was the lucky one.

Another year went by, and this time I was on the top of the totem pole. I was a senior in high school, and the world was there for the taking. Channel 3, based out of Cleveland, was doing a series of stories profiling people who had been through a lot in their lives, focusing on recovery and inspirational stories. I was one of those stories and was incredibly lucky to have that attention, because it was my first chance to help others.

In addition to that, one of the most incredible feelings I can remember from high school occurred in the spring of 1993. It was for the league track meet. Willard was part of the Northern Ohio League, and my focus was the 800-meter run. All year long I had been training for the event, winning some, losing some, but for someone who, only a couple of years prior, was given two weeks to live, I was doing really well.

Warming up for the event, I was running back and forth inside the track on the football field. High knees, butt kicks, long strides, skipping, stretching, the works. I was ready to go. They called us down to the end of the 100-meter race area, and we all jogged past the stands on our right to the start of the 800-meter run. Jumping up and kicking my heels together straight up and down, shaking out my thighs, I was getting ready and loose.

My teammate was in the same lane as me. There were eight lanes and sixteen total runners, each representing his school. I hunched over, said a short prayer, and got up for the race. After I warmed up, sweat trickled down my forehead and my chin, dripping onto the track. It wasn't a hot day, but it wasn't cold. It was overcast and cool, my favorite kind of day.

"Runners, set!" *Bang*. The gun went off, and I had two laps ahead of me to run. Turning the first corner in lane six, I couldn't see the others behind me, only the four runners in lanes seven and eight. Hitting the backstretch, I kept my stride long and fast and my arms loose; I felt great. The second turn, the other runners were catching up to me and passing me, coming up to the front stretch in front of the stands, where everyone was standing to cheer us on. We made one lap, and something snapped. Not in my leg, not in my ankle. Nowhere on my body but in my head. I wanted this race. I was going to own this race. I was going to win.

It was the same thing that had happened when I was battling cancer and told myself I wasn't going to get sick again, that I wasn't going to vomit anymore. I was going to win. I knew in my soul and in the back of my mind that it was mine. I turned the corner and started pushing harder. My strides got longer, stronger, and more powerful. On the backstretch, I started passing people and reeling them in like fish. I felt incredible and was running with (of all things) a smile on my face.

The smile might have been a bit premature, but if you're not having fun, what are you out there for, right? There were a few more people I still had to get in front of me. We were rounding the last corner, and I was running on the outside. I knew what Coach had told us: "Never run on the outside, because it's a lot longer and it'll suck your energy." I didn't care. I was passing people on the outside while they were running the shorter, easier inside part of the track.

With the last corner over and the last 100-meter homestretch left, I was in the lead. Never looking over my shoulder but kicking it in high gear, I knew I was leaving everyone behind me and was going to win. Everyone was left in the dust while I kept getting faster and faster. I crossed the line, hands up in the air, with my first finger pointing to the sky, saying, "Number one!"

I did it! I won my high school's league track meet in the 800-meter run. And to think, only a couple of years earlier, I was in a medical-induced coma, bedridden, learning to breathe again because I had my ribs cracked open so the surgeons could remove the tumor. Now here I was, running against some of the best athletes in the state of Ohio and winning.

CHAPTER EIGHT

THE $100,000 PARTY

❖

All during my senior year of high school, like most kids (God, how I loved being like most kids), I was applying to a number of different colleges and universities, all with swim teams and track teams. To keep my options open, I looked at a number of small schools as well as large ones. Dad drove me around on my few free weekends from swimming, track, and my burgeoning social life to visit the schools, meet the coaches, see the students, the campuses, and the admissions folks. When the whole admissions process was all said and done, I had applied to seven schools and was accepted into every one of them. Pretty good, if I do say so myself.

After visiting the schools, I decided on one about two and a half hours away from home (sometimes I think I made it home in about an hour and forty-five minutes). It was finally official: Westminster College was going to be my home for the next four years. I saw this as more than a new leg of my educational journey. If you think about it (and you can bet I did), this was an incredible way for me to start over.

Not a single person there knew who I was, what I had been through, where I'd come from, or anything. There was none of the baggage that had followed me through the halls of junior high or high school. No one would be seeing the new Sean or the old

Sean or the thin Sean or the fat Sean or the wig Sean or the sick Sean; they would simply be seeing Sean.

I was starting with a clean slate and could write my own future. I was excited to get going and start my new life with my new roommate, but I was a little hesitant at first. He was from Hoboken, New Jersey, about a twenty-minute ferry ride from Manhattan. Great. I was going to be living with some big-city slicker. Here I was, from a town of about five thousand people, and he was leaving his home of over a million. Through phone calls and letters (we didn't have the Internet yet), I found that he seemed like a nice enough guy, and after getting used to the idea, I wasn't as worried about it. Turned out Brendan and I were roommates throughout our entire college career and, better yet, became best friends in the process.

Freshman year was fantastic, but little did I know Mom and Dad had talked to the swim coach, as well as Brendan, because they were worried about me. I found out much later that they had approached both of them and told them my medical history. Sneaky as can be, yes. Was I upset about it when I found out? Oh, you bet! But when the dust cleared and my temper tantrum blew over, I could see why it made sense to them. After all, they weren't sure I was going to make it through college alive. Not because I was going to do something stupid, like jump off the rafters into the water, or drink myself into oblivion, or try some things I shouldn't have—I did all that *and* survived. No, they couldn't know if I was going to remain cancer-free for the next four years.

They had good cause to doubt me: The magical number was five years, and if I could make it through that, I was pretty much in remission. If I could make it ten years, the science held, then I was officially cancer-free and in remission for the rest of my life. Mom and Dad were nervous, and if either the coach or my roommate saw something off kilter, they were to let Mom or Dad know immediately. I still think that was over the top, and overprotective, but it also shows love for a son from his parents.

I made many friends, had a number of girlfriends, and lived life to the fullest. I started off my freshman year studying molecular biology. Hey, it made sense to me: I was going to play God and change genes. Cure cancer through genetic engineering. That lasted all the way to my junior year, until I took immunology and organic chemistry. (Yuck.) That was enough of that.

During the same time, I was taking an introduction to psychology class. I loved it. I changed my major from molecular biology to psychology. Much better. This time I was going to be a psychologist for cancer patients and their families. Like many college students, I wasn't worried about what I would do with that future phrase, "the rest of my life." I was living in the university bubble, and my only focus was on the immediate. What I needed now, not later, was what mattered. Parties? Oh, good Lord, you bet. I didn't just go to parties; I was the original party animal. I was plucked from the movie *Animal House*. If there was a party, I was there. Sometimes even dressed up in a funky outfit. (Perhaps all that wig wearing was finally paying off.)

Looking back at this one fraternity party I went to, I still laugh at myself and roll my eyes. Westminster College didn't have any bars to go to, so we didn't have need for fake IDs. We would get our booze from our upperclassman friends. Simple. Also, because there was nothing else to do at school, over 70 percent of the student population was involved in the Greek system. So when I say I used to go to fraternity parties, it's not like a lot of the larger universities, and don't get a bad taste in your mouth or a sour look on your face, because the people at the frats were nice, open, caring, and above all, fun.

For the frat party in question, I decided I wanted to have a little fun. (Scratch that; a little more fun than usual.) I found a Mickey Mouse hat, you know the one: the *Fantasia* wizard's hat. Wore it. I also found some goggles from our swim team. Wore those, too. And to top off the entire outfit, we had these little red flippers for swimming called Zoomers. Wore those as well.

Flopping around the fraternity house looking like I belonged in a mental institution, I had an incredible time, not worried about what a single person thought of me. Why should I worry? I was alive, and this was my chance at a new start, a new life. Did I want to be the cancer boy on campus? No. Did I want to be known as the fragile guy who didn't have any fun? Oh, God, no. I wanted to be known as the party animal, the friendly guy, the person everyone could relate to. I'll never forget something one of my friends said while talking to a group of people about me: "I wish I was like Sean. He drinks and sobers up!"

That's right—I was the wild one zipping around campus, through the classrooms, the halls, all while wearing my new in-line skates. I was poetry in motion, going up and down steps, over whatever was in my way. A joke spread around campus that I slept in those things. I can't tell you how many times I got in trouble with the professors for wearing them indoors, but every time they said something, I'd make up an answer, like "Oh, don't worry, they're indoor/outdoor wheels."

I was the guy swinging from the rafters during parties, peeing off balconies into the lawn if the bathroom wait was too long. (Or even if it wasn't.) I couldn't get enough of life. Granted, I shouldn't have done some of the things, but it was college, and I was living my life and, at the same time, reliving high school. I had never been invited to any big parties at Willard, so when I hit Westminster, I was an animal come out of hiding, a bear come out of hibernation. I became the beer pong king (a drinking game involving two Ping-Pong balls, ten cups on either side of a table, and, well, you do the math) and a rock star.

My grades? Let's not talk about those, okay? (Or, as I used to say at Westminster, "Why be a buzz kill?") How about I just say I should have picked up a book every now and then as opposed to the night before an exam? And sometimes I didn't even do that. However, if I had to go back and do it all over again (like everything in line with my life philosophy), I wouldn't change a thing.

Of course, it wasn't all fun and games: Swimming in college was different than swimming in high school. Way different. When I was on the team in high school, I trained at another pool (my high school didn't have a pool) and with the YMCA and USS teams. We'd practice once a day for about an hour and a half. College? Good Lord. We'd be up, on deck, and in the water every morning at six A.M. for at least two hours. After classes, we'd go back in for at least two more. So in one day, we'd practice at least four hours.

When I was there, we were part of the NAIA (National Association for Intercollegiate Athletics) and not the NCAA (National Collegiate Athletic Association), so we didn't have to abide by any collegiate-wide rules limiting our practice hours. I'd pray for a lab or an extension in class so I wouldn't have to go to practice. (Which, if you'll recall my academic philosophy from this time period, is saying a lot.) For whatever reason, I never got any better in swimming. Maybe because the surgery to remove the tumor from my second cancer also damaged—and partially re-moved—my latissimus dorsi muscle (back muscle). I had a left one, but the right one was hardly there.

Pull-ups? Ha. Forget it. I looked so lopsided, it wasn't even funny. So when I hit college and tried to get better, faster, stronger, it wasn't there. My freestyle times were staying around the same as when I was seventeen or eighteen, even in my sopho-more year and early junior years. I wasn't lugging around any extra weight, so what was it?

I asked my doctors about it, and they told me I would never get my endurance back. They also said that I'd never really be fit again and that I should be happy where I was. What, were they new here? That certainly wasn't going to happen. Not if I had anything to do with it. So I continued swimming and working my tail off, trying to get faster, better, stronger, but with no positive results.

I kept getting the same times, and my personal bests would be only a little faster, if that. No matter how hard I worked, nothing seemed to be making me any faster. I didn't understand it, and frankly, I couldn't handle it very well. After all, this was supposed to be my comeback story, my second act, the prime of my life. Rocky wasn't supposed to lose in the final round. How could this be happening?

After a while, I succumbed to the doctors' notions. Or maybe I just needed a break from swimming and thought I'd get back into it later in my life, which I did in my first triathlon, where I went into the water around four hundredth place, only to come out in thirteenth. Maybe all I needed was a break.

Each summer when I went back home (my parents moved

from Willard to Sandusky while I was in college so my brother could swim on a real team), life became more and more incredible. I wasn't even thinking about my cancers, how they affected my life or anything negative. Life was one big joyride for me, and summer only put the pedal to the metal.

I never got carded when buying beer as an underager (as long as I didn't shave for about a week beforehand) and sometimes worked five different jobs a day. I might get up and coach a local swim team at four-thirty A.M., then go over to another club team and coach there as the swim coach and dive coach. After that I'd hang around and lifeguard. After guarding was over, I'd don the red-and-white-striped shirt of T.G.I. Friday's and fulfill one of any number of job descriptions they had to offer.

I started off as what they called a "smiling people greeter." Yeah, get your chuckles out now, I know it's funny. After that I worked up to busboy, bar-back, waiter (I think I did that for about three days), bar float, and finally, the big honcho—bartender. Me? A bartender? In Sandusky, Ohio? (Sandusky was an incredible place of wild parties, girls, and booze.) It was like letting a fox into the chicken coop.

It's easy to extrapolate that all four of my college years were a wreck. An utter bomb of a party and a delirium that was, in a word, fantastic. I loved every minute of being alive and having no fear. While in college, I fell in love every week but managed to keep my head on straight through the four and a half years I was there. Yup. I was one of the lucky ones who managed to put off the real world for a little while longer.

Because I changed my major so late in college, I had to hang around for an extra term, all for one class. It was my senior thesis class, which was offered only in the fall term and on Wednesdays only. Party time, for sure! I was in college for one class? Are you kidding me? I lived above four girls that year in the same house, and we all spent too much time on the other end of a beer can. We played so many drinking games and had such an incredible time, we thought we were turning into alcoholics. Seriously. We had to come up with a reason to celebrate on Wednesday nights so we could justify it to ourselves and not feel guilty.

I also helped coach the swim team. I couldn't participate in either track or swimming because my eligibility had run out (I did both sports in college), but I felt a loyalty to the team. The swim season ran into the late winter/early spring, so I stayed at school until it was over. In the meantime, that thing I'd been avoiding for four and a half years—a little thing the rest of the world calls life—really kicked me in the groin.

College was over. What was I going to do now? Well, my thoughts were to get into a doctoral program and become a psychologist for cancer patients. *Man,* I thought, at the time, *that's a lot of hard work!* But I knew I was ready for it. I knew that was what I wanted to do, so I took the GRE and applied to a number of schools in England. They all had highly accredited programs where I could get my doctoral degree in about four years. Believe it or not, I was accepted into all of those programs because my GRE score was incredibly high. I was even told (not sure if it was true or not) that my score was the highest to ever come out of the psychology department of my school. I'm sure most, if not all, of the professors were taken aback, since I graduated with a GPA of under 3.0. Like I said, I never studied. But when I put my mind to it, I did well on the entrance exam.

After being accepted into all those schools overseas, I discovered there were no grants or scholarships to support the nearly

$30,000 tuition. Back to square one. I had a couple of choices. I could work and wait until the next winter to go to school, or I could get my butt in gear and apply to more schools now. I went with the latter option.

I applied to a number of schools in the South because I was tired of the cold weather and snow. (Kind of ironic, looking back at that decision, huh?) I ended up going to school in Florida. In one week I was accepted into the University of North Florida and on my way south from Ohio. I was leaving my friends behind and venturing into uncharted waters. I had no idea what it would be like, who my roommate was, or anything. Though my Westminster roommate, Brendan, had turned out to be a pleasant surprise, my welcome in the Sunshine State was anything but bright.

One of my roommates was a pothead who sold dope out of the apartment and did steroids and other drugs. I moved into another apartment where my new roommates did coke. Nice view of Florida so far, huh? I did learn to surf and managed to make a few friends, some of whom were on the swim team I helped coach. Again, I always tried to look on the bright side of things and smiled as much as I could.

At this point in my life, I was changing directions. I was getting a 4.0 in school, but that wasn't enough for me. For some reason, I felt like I didn't belong. Almost the entire time I was in Florida, it was like sleepwalking through a period that was neither a dream nor a nightmare. I was just existing, going through the motions because I'd come too far to go back and never felt whole enough to put down roots where I was.

My life never seemed to be real, and I never once felt like I was myself. I wasn't the fun-loving, worry-free Sean. I was the responsible, working three jobs to put myself through grad school, uptight Sean. It wasn't fun, and worse yet, I wasn't fun. I was working as a head bartender at one of the most popular clubs on the beach, but that didn't do it for me.

I didn't like the hurricanes we had to dodge, nor did I like moving everything I owned in my Honda Civic to Gainesville because we were under mandatory evacuation. I did like the times I was by myself, running in the woods being chased by horseflies. They were my motivation to keep running, to keep going, and to keep moving forward. Horseflies or no, I was getting tired of this place and fast.

I applied to some more schools and was accepted into a doctoral program in Chicago. Long story short. I was no longer in the master's program in Florida, and I finally did some thinking about my life. A thousand miles away from my mom and dad in Ohio, and Seth in Pennsylvania. Grandma and Grandpa lived in Orlando, and I visited them a number of times, but other than that, I was alone. Me against the world. Or, more appropriate, me against myself. I felt like I was missing something. I felt like I had unresolved issues to deal with now that the constant partying of college was behind me.

I guess it was to be expected. For most of junior high and high school, I had been either getting treatments for my cancers or in remission, so it was a constant emotional roller coaster that I could never stop. In college, my life was for the living; the cancer was behind me, and there was no day but today. Now there was only the future, and I had to start facing facts. I had to find out what I could do that would not only help me but help others feel like I felt: grateful to be alive.

I knew something was wrong. Maybe the Sunshine State wasn't a total wash after all. Florida was the first place I did some thinking about my life and about what had happened to me. About the C-word that had been a part of my life for such a long time, and about that part of life I shoved under the carpet for the four and a half years of my college career.

Even while dating someone, I was afraid to tell her about my past. I was afraid it would scare her away. I kept it a secret for such a long time. Why should I be embarrassed about it? I did nothing to get it. I'm not weak or anything like that. It just happened. I thought I had covered this when I was thirteen, going through the first cancer. I thought I had worked out everything that was in my head.

Apparently not. Apparently, it was still with me, and I had some huge baggage to deal with. I never went to any group therapy sessions, but I wish they'd been available to me. I would have known I wasn't alone. I would have had someone to talk to about the entire ordeal, and probably would have felt better, not only about myself but about the entire situation and experience.

So here I was, battling myself. This internal struggle tearing at me. I'd be sitting at a red light, staring at the license plate in front of me, in a zone until the car behind me honked. The light was green, and who knew how long I was sitting there, staring into space. Something was wrong for sure.

This was when I took off and started running again and made friends with the horseflies. God knows if I stopped or slowed down, those buggers would make a meal out of my naked back. Somewhere while running in the woods, I had an epiphany: Cancer is a part of my life. I did nothing to get it, but it is a part of me. It does not describe who I am, nor does it define me as a person, but it definitely has helped me become who I am now, and I must accept that. I must accept, not understand, but *know* cancer has made me who I am.

With that in mind, I knew I wanted to do what I could to help inspire others around the world who had been touched by cancer. To give them hope. To bring to the table the C-word and let countless people understand that it's okay to have cancer, and it's okay to be sick with it. It's also okay to battle through. And for those who wouldn't make it, I wanted to do what I could to give them the little glimmer of hope they deserved and needed while they were fighting for their lives. When I was battling cancer, I had no one to look up to. I wanted to give those people something, to do something for as many people as possible. What? That part I wasn't sure about. I just knew I wanted to do something, and that something would have to be huge.

Around the same time, Seth was finishing up college, and my parents and I went to see him graduate. It was a fantastic time, seeing him walk down the grassy aisle with his diploma, taking his photo, smiling like a million bucks. I was so proud of him that day. He eventually moved down to South Carolina to live with Mom and Dad for a while. (After I'd been in Florida for two years, Mom and Dad had moved there to be closer to me. Or so they say—I think they got sick of the cold, too.)

When Seth moved down there, he spent a lot of time living with me and helping me with a number of ideas. First I thought I was going to run across the country to raise money. Too much running. Then I thought I could do marathons in every big city around the U.S. Again, too much running.

What was I thinking? I wanted big. Bigger. Huge, like I'd decided before. I wanted Everest. Even though I had no climbing experience, I wanted the highest platform in the world to proclaim the potential of the human body and spirit. I wanted to shout from the rooftop of the world that there is hope, that there truly is no mountain too high to climb, literally and figuratively. With Seth's help, I discovered that if I could make it to the summit of the world's highest mountain, I'd become the first cancer survivor in history to make the epic journey.

What better platform than the highest peak on earth?

And that's exactly what I was going to do.

CHAPTER NINE

ICE AXE SHISH KEBAB

❖

After my decision to "climb for cancer," my brother, Seth, and I founded (appropriately enough) the CancerClimber Association. Like most things my brother and I started, it was a joint effort from the very beginning. CancerClimber was founded to fund cancer research, but over time we changed our mission statement because we believed there were plenty of people out there funding research already. We wanted to make a difference now and not years down the road.

Today we give grants to cancer survivors to inspire cancer patients through their own events and personal challenges. These survivors give hope to patients by doing something amazing and then visiting local hospitals to tell their personal stories. We have a sleek new website and lots of news to post. Back then we were a little more grassroots. We knew we wanted to do something worthwhile, we just weren't quite sure what that might be yet.

Although Seth was lucky enough to be cancer-free, he had grown up with cancer. Like most brothers, though, we didn't talk about it much. There were a lot of questions unasked and unanswered. Did he resent my getting all the attention while we were growing up? Did he miss the time we would have spent together if I hadn't gotten sick?

As we started the foundation, his actions spoke for themselves. It was inspiring for me to see how passionate he was about the organization, and I knew how right I'd been not only to decide to climb for cancer but to enlist Seth as my equal partner in the new venture. I knew that whatever we decided to do with the organization, it would be a chance to make up for lost time and do something together.

Once he set up a website and we got all the other details in order, Seth and I decided it was time to break the news to Mom and Dad—in our own unique way. We put them in front of the computer, pointed them to the website, and went to have a beer while they explored on their own. It was a Swarner tradition: confrontation-free. Eventually, we heard whispers, chatter, and then our father's stern voice as he bellowed, "Boys, get up here."

Mom and Dad have always been supportive of everything I've ever done. They may not have agreed with it, but regardless, they have been incredible with their unconditional support over the years. If I wanted to try something, they were there to catch me if I fell. Luckily, I never did, but they were the safety net that allowed me such freedom to fly.

This time was a little different. Mom and Dad were thrilled that we wanted to do something positive surrounding cancer, but there were practical considerations. Where would we live? How would we earn a living? Who would put a roof over our heads and bread in our bellies?

As it happened, the unveiling of the website ended in a draw. Our folks were impressed with what we'd accomplished but concerned about all of the practical applications we hadn't nailed down. As for Seth and me we were glad the cat was out of the bag and eager to get on the road. But where? Obviously, we couldn't live in Florida or South Carolina, because you can't train for Everest in board shorts and sandals on fifteen-foot sand dunes. Maybe

Mom and Dad were right after all. Here we were, making the decision to climb the world's tallest mountain, and we couldn't even decide on the best place to train.

I started doing a lot of research on the phone, over the Internet, and at the library, because it dawned on me that we were making some huge decisions in our lives. Hours passed into days before we decided to make Colorado our home. When we factored everything in, it seemed like the logical choice. Colorado had plenty of mountains for training, it was accessible and affordable, and it didn't hurt that the state boasted a certain kind of climbing culture. We needed to go where we belonged, where we'd fit in and people wouldn't look at us funny for training 24-7.

Even so, settling on Colorado was one of the biggest leaps of faith I ever took, because I had no experience with climbing. Swimming, sure. Track, yes. Rocks and peaks and thousand-foot drops? Not so much. But that was the point: I was confident I would get experience in the Rocky Mountains. I had to.

So it was settled. Colorado, here we come. I was nervous because my training, not to mention the climb itself, would mean taking a sabbatical from my studies and putting my life on hold for the next 365 days. It was a scary thought, and there was a point when I could have choked and gone either way. In the end, I knew moving to Colorado and testing my limits in the Rocky Mountains was the choice I'd made when I decided to reach out to the world with my story.

Seth and I had no place to live after we decided we had to get to Colorado to train for my first climb. So it was back to the drawing board: more phone calls, more hours spent on the Internet, more dumb luck. Before departing South Carolina, I managed to get in touch with a number of companies that pledged their support in this dream of putting the first cancer survivor on top of the world.

Boots, trekking poles, backpacks, clothing, GPS: I made calls to countless companies over and over again. I was a lot more familiar with the sound of the dial tone after the phone hung up then I was with hearing "yes." Think about it—you're in charge of a huge company's PR and marketing departments, you get a call from a two-time cancer survivor with only one fully functioning lung, living in one of the flattest states in the country, saying he's climbing the world's highest mountain. Oh, and by the way, that Everest climber has little to no experience. Won't you please donate to his cause?

In addition to the companies, there were a few individuals who were there to help do what they could with what they had. Before packing up and moving sight unseen to Colorado, I'd gotten in touch with a group who owned a campsite out in Estes Park, Colorado. They were willing to let Seth and me camp under McGregor Slab for as long as we needed.

After the initial chats about what we were going to do, how we were going to live, and what was going to happen (all with the resounding answer of "I have no idea, but it'll get done for sure," which, by the way, became CancerClimber's unofficial motto), Seth and I packed up my Civic (called Pepe) and headed out.

The day was Tuesday, July 17.

In my mind, that will always be day one of the Everest climb.

The day started out with me hearing my brother showering in the next bedroom. Next thing I knew, our dad walked in, crying. He hugged me goodbye and told me to be careful and wished me good luck and told me how much he'd miss me.

All of this was before five A.M.

I tried to fall back asleep, but it was pointless. I'd had a rough night's sleep, tossing and turning; I was so anxious for this day to get here, this day that I'd been waiting on forever. This day that I had foreseen but had never contemplated, not really. I'd just known it was going to happen. I was starting my life and heading out into the world, scared to death of the unknown. I got out of bed and tossed in my eyeballs (contacts), got breakfast, and took care of some things I hadn't finished the night before. Most of the packing was done, and all the stuff from my apartment in Jacksonville was stowed away in Mom and Dad's attic.

Breakfast consisted of eggs and waffles. After Seth and I moved my gigantic picture of James Dean into the attic, we packed up our personal stuff (e.g., toothbrushes), then said goodbye to Mom. Much like our parting words with dear old Dad, this wasn't going to be easy. She was so choked up, she could barely speak.

"Take good care of each other, be careful, good luck. I'll be praying for you." All those good things came out through muffled sobs and a boxful of tissues. We left as soon as we could, not to be callous but to avoid any more waterworks. As soon as we hit the road outside the driveway, I started getting choked up and said to Seth, "Dude, this sucks." Seth agreed, and we settled in for the long haul.

It's always tough leaving the ones you love, but it must be done someday, and what better way than chasing after a dream this immense? The trip was relatively quiet (that's what happens when you hit the road by five-thirty in the morning) until I said, "We need gas." We also talked about how Mom must be bawling back at home and how I hated hurting other people. (I'm sure I'll find out how bad it is whenever I have kids.)

After filling up, we hopped back into the car, and Seth was busy opening up some game pieces he had picked up at the station—his first one was "You win a Mustang!" Both of us were ecstatic until we saw at the same time a bunch of numbers you had to match to win it. We *did* win a hot dog, coffee, and a doughnut, though. What better way to start a drive from South Carolina to Colorado, right?

Things were already looking up.

From there, the trip started in earnest, a patchwork odyssey to chase our dreams. We had no reservations at fancy hotels or deadlines to meet. Like strangers at a potluck dinner, we had lined up lodging with an odd assortment of family and friends along the way. There were no traveler's checks or guidebooks, just a couple of brothers fighting over the radio in a cramped little car.

Our first day brought us from Mom and Dad's place in South Carolina to a campsite in Alabama. (No hotels for us; after all, CancerClimber was a nonprofit organization.) The second day we ended up in Memphis to stay with one of Seth's friends. The third, we stopped at the house of a friend in Kansas who had battled cancer herself and was doing everything she could to help us with our dream. Our cousin lived in Denver at the time, so that was our next and last stop before making Estes Park and McGregor Slab, our official home for training.

Obviously, we were hoping to have some sort of warmth before the first snow, but at this altitude and at night, we weren't sure that was going to happen. I made a halfhearted joke about snow tires and chains, but for all I knew, we might need both. We moved to Estes Park with no real plan, just a dream in mind and a mountain in sight. I was lucky enough that Seth had recently graduated from college and was willing to help me with this dream.

For his part, Seth seemed content to be part of the adventure. Not even the luxury of hindsight can make us look back on that odyssey and call it a little slice of heaven on earth—try being cramped up with your brother for most of a business week—but it was one of the first times we'd ever been forced to sit and communicate. "Bonding" might be a strong word for what happened along the way, but it fits nonetheless. We started the trip as brothers; we ended it as friends.

When we rolled into Estes Park on the fifth day, we were greeted with majestic views of the Colorado Rockies as we ascended into the sleepy mountain town at 7,522 feet above sea level. Lake Estes is the central feature of this typical climbing village, where campers, climbers, trekkers, and locals live side by side with nature. It seemed a fitting place to set up camp.

Our site was just below the north entrance of Rocky Mountain National Park, with a winding and very steep entrance. After winding up through lush fir trees on the gravel road, we came to a stop at one of the highest sites on the reservation.

Our meager belongings didn't quite match the majestic surroundings. We didn't even have a decent tent to sleep in, just one of those small, flimsy pup tents, kind of like a sheet draped over a stick in the shape of an A. (I think we'd had better accommodations playing fort in the family living room when we were kids.) We did have another, larger tent, but that was for storage of all our equipment, because we needed Pepe (remember the car?) for errands, groceries, and other things.

To say that we lived out of the back of my car for a while would be an understatement. We lived out of the back of the car, some tents, and cooked our food over an open fire in the middle of our campsite. Most of the time we didn't have hot dinners, only sandwiches. Once in a while we'd experiment by putting tuna in mac and cheese. Nutrition? We had no idea what that meant, because we couldn't afford it.

I think the local Boy Scouts would have been better prepared for roughing it than we were, but that didn't stop us from waking each morning with a smile and a quick glance at the mountains that surrounded us. Anyone can walk into a sporting goods store and splurge on the best tent in stock. We were at the starting line of the most important race either of us had ever run; that was all that mattered.

For weeks, Seth and I would wake up, go for a hike, and then head into town to the local library, where we would search for more sponsors and more funding, more ideas and ways to make this dream come alive. We had already established the nonprofit organization, CancerClimber, and were out soliciting donations to support the expedition, give back to research, and help others by giving hope and inspiration to those fighting for their lives.

One idea Mom had was to collect names of people who were touched by cancer (currently battling it, in remission, or passed away), put them on a flag, and take that flag up to the top of the world or as high as I could get. We originally talked to a marketing group about charging a hundred or more dollars per name, but that never seemed quite right to me. That wasn't the idea: getting your name on this flag as a privilege only a few could afford. The idea was to offer it to anyone, regardless of what they could afford. So we decided that thirty bucks to get a name on the flag would be fair enough; they could help fund the climb that would, we hoped, in turn fund future climbs to raise even more awareness. It seemed like a good investment in all of our futures. A photo of the flag on the summit, and some inspirational words from me, would be our way of thanking those people for their support.

In a way, we'd all be making the climb together.

Aside from the funding, sponsorship, and products we had to get, I also had to train for the hardest endurance event my body had ever faced. Like battling cancer, it would be a challenging, uphill struggle. Unlike battling cancer, it would be a tad more public.

Seth and I were *still* living in a tent and out of the back of my car. It might sound rustic or romantic even (if I'd been sharing it with a cute girl), but it wasn't conducive to the kind of high-impact, high-stress training I needed to accomplish. We needed ultimate conditions, not bottom end. However, I couldn't let a small thing like no housing stop me from achieving that dream. The first mountain I climbed was Longs Peak in Rocky Mountain National Park. Packing the night before was fun, since we knew little about this trek, except for some information from a topographic map Seth had printed off the Internet in the library.

Gear? We didn't have any but the boots and stuff we'd brought with us from home. All we knew was that the peak was about 14,256 feet high. We also heard from the people we talked to around the camp site that we had to start climbing/hiking at about two-thirty in the morning to avoid the horrible thunderstorms that swing through like clockwork at one P.M. every day. So when we packed, we had no idea what we were getting into. Eventually, we packed two gallons of water, two windbreakers, twenty granola bars, beef stew, a machete, and went to bed.

A machete? What were we thinking?

That night I kept tossing and turning because of the anticipation. We were going to get up at two-fifty and leave at three in the morning. One A.M. rolled around, and Seth said, "Dude, let's go."

I mumbled back, "Give me twenty minutes, then wake me up and we'll go." I was hoping he would fall asleep. Five minutes later, I couldn't sleep, either, so I sat up and said, "Screw it, let's go!" We didn't have any money to buy headlamps, nor did we have a sponsor for them yet, so I taped our LED flashlights to the side of our baseball hats. (That worked great, believe it or not.)

We hopped in the car and headed out. On the way there, we passed a fox and what looked like either a wolf or a coyote. We were pretty sure it was a coyote. It was 9.2 miles up Route 7, so when we hit that, we turned right and headed up the windy road. When we got to the trailhead, we loaded up our backs and said hello to a few other people getting ready. Then we took off up the mountain.

We signed the logbook at precisely two-thirty A.M. and took off up the mountain with our lights duct-taped to our noggins like some prehistoric miners. Good Lord, what a motley sight we must have been. The first part of the climb was supposed to be a trail through some lush trees and then a wasteland—a high alpine tundra, a boulder field with rocks the size of cars, and the keyhole, a tiny gateway from the east side of the mountain to the west, and the rest of the route to the summit. Despite the late hour and surrounding darkness, we were keeping a good pace, singing out loud, trying to keep each other awake. I would lead for a while, and Seth would lead for a while, and when it was wide enough, we would walk side by side. Walking behind him sucked, to be honest. The only scenery I could see were boots, the ground, and a butt.

In the woods, we caught up with some people who had stopped to put on more clothing or change water. We joked, "Hey, when you pass us, just poke us and shoo away the buzzards. Would ya?" They chuckled and we kept going. A little way up, I pulled out the topo Seth had printed and tried to figure out where the hell we were on the trail. Right around dawn, we took a break and sat down to watch the sun crack over the horizon. Climbers see a lot of sunrises and sunsets over the course of their lives; call it a perk of the job. With all the sunrises I've seen, before or since, I can honestly say that was one of the most beautiful I've ever witnessed. Sharing that moment with my brother—with our lives stretched out in front of us and one gigantic mountain to train for—was confirmation that all was right in our world. I didn't care how high I was going, and I didn't care that we were only a few days out from sea level. I knew this was the right thing to do with my life.

Heading up the last section of the climb, called the Homestretch (after the keyhole), we were behind a few people going rather slowly. I couldn't blame them; despite the cozy name, the section is a long, slate face where, if you slipped, you'd slide a couple of thousand feet to your death.

I was following a petite woman who happened to misstep and started sliding down the face. Without even thinking, just reacting, I stretched out my arm and grabbed the lip of her backpack with a couple of fingers and managed to stop her from sliding down to her death. Lucky for me, she was pretty tiny, and I had a good grip on the rock.

Nothing much was said or done about the incident. Things like that happen all the time; you just brush yourself off, manage a breathless "thanks," and move on. About twenty minutes later,

Seth and I were standing on the summit of my first climb, cracking a celebratory beer and breaking out the Doritos. Like so many of my climbs, this one had all the elements: life, death, and Doritos.

Looking back, I can honestly say I loved every minute of it. I started to get teary-eyed, touching the brass emblem marking the height—the highest I'd ever been. We signed the summit log, got our pictures taken by some of the folks who were also up there, and got ready for the hike home.

The clouds started rolling in, and I could see the tops of them hiking back down into the boulder field. On the way back through the trees, nearly back to the parking lot about eighteen miles into the round-trip hike, we discovered why it was called "Longs" Peak. We were so exhausted from the distance, I swear I saw the parking lot on the side of the mountain in the middle of the woods. Okay, maybe I was hallucinating, seeing cars in the forest, but whatever it was, we weren't acclimated to the altitude, that's for sure.

After the incredibly long mini-expedition, we knew we needed to find a place to live, and fast. Colorado weather at 8,500 feet isn't like Florida, and all we had were some cheap sleeping bags from our childhood when we'd camp in the backyard. A pay phone on the campground became my office. I spent hours standing around at the lodge, using that pay phone, and trying to get people and companies interested in helping our cause. So far I'd managed to convince several companies to help out with some gear and was having a conversation with Cabela's, a legendary name in the world of outdoor training and a major corporation.

Finding support for the climb was like making friends with the most popular kid at school; once I could start dropping a name like Cabela's, the floodgates practically opened for us. KAVU, LEKI, Asolo, Mountainsmith, Misty Mountain, Brunton, and Suunto all jumped on the support wagon and were behind the idea and dream from Florida on. All incredible people, and I can't thank them enough for believing in me and supporting us from the word go. From them we received climbing clothing, training clothes, trekking poles, boots, backpacks, harnesses, GPS equipment, and wrist computers (elaborate watches with altitude, barometer, compass, etc). No more LED lights strapped onto ball caps for Seth and me. In the immortal words of the Jeffersons, we were "moving on up."

Training became a holistic blend of body and mind. The mountain worked my body; the fund-raising worked my mind. For the longest time, the days consisted of us waking up, me going for a run or a hike, driving into town to use the library computers to check e-mail, driving "home" to begin the calls from the pay phone, trying to convince people and companies to help. This went on for countless days.

Word spread, we got in touch with the right people, and eventually, things started looking up. Especially when I swung in to talk to a place called the Evergreens on Fall River, an establishment renting satellite cabins. Keeley, the woman behind the counter that fateful day, looked a little confused when I started asking her whom I should talk to about living arrangements and how I could go about getting a place to stay. I explained the situation, told her my story, directed her to the CancerClimber website, and essentially pleaded my cause. It so happened that their house was on the property and they had a basement apartment where the cleaning staff usually lived. They were heading into the slow season and had a room open. It was a two-bedroom apartment with a kitchen that was below their house. She told me to come back in a few days and she'd have a decision for me.

The stars were shining bright that day, and someone from above was looking kindly down upon us. Seth and I moved into a stable shelter, had a phone, two beds in one of the bedrooms, and a kitchen. It wasn't much, but the family became our best sponsor and, in turn, like our family away from home. We couldn't have been any luckier. We lent a hand around the satellite cabins they rented and cleaned the places for them in exchange for a place to stay. They became such an integral part to our training and support, I don't know if we could have completed the climb without them.

I remember the first meal Seth and I cooked on a real stove with a roof over our head: ramen noodles and beef stew. Yum. From there we would launch our training. It would be our office, our home base, our chow hall, our research lab, our cooking school, and our training center, where we'd run up and down countless peaks in the Rocky Mountains.

Training consisted of something way out of the ordinary. The woman we had stayed with in Kansas had given us more than shelter for a night; she had given me a book on mountaineering, climbing, and other rock sports, and from that I derived a training plan in the usual Sean Swarner way. I did a lot of research, talked to a lot of people, and set something down to make a training schedule that was unique to me. I would do some sort of activity nearly every day leading up to the Everest expedition. Be it running, hiking, going up and down the stairs with two hundred pounds of rocks in my backpack (come to think of it, I bet I'd be about an inch taller if I hadn't done that), or hiking up a 14,000-foot peak with a hundred pounds of rocks, I knew I had to be in the best shape of my life to make the summit of Everest. I also knew I was going to be controversial because of my lack of climbing ability/skills. I had absolutely no high-altitude experience.

That's why I also tried to organize a trip up a mountain in Tibet called Cho Oyu. It was a 26,000-foot-plus mountain and would give me a good idea how I would cope at such a high altitude and how my body would react above the 8,000-meter mark. (That mark is also known as the Death Zone, which we'll get to later in the book, but I'm guessing you can figure out just from the name that it's not such a comfortable place to be.) Unfortunately, that trip never happened because the funding wasn't there, so it would be a complete guess as to how my body was going to react in the altitude of Everest.

After a good few months of gaining a base in my training, I hiked back up Longs Peak, this time with about a hundred pounds of rocks in my pack. My thought was that if I could carry a hundred pounds at 14,000 feet, I could carry thirty pounds at 26,000 feet. It also gave my legs an incredible workout and helped me develop amazing stamina. Not only did I carry tremendous amounts of weights in the altitude, I wore shorts and postholed (basically stomping through the snow when it's a few feet deep) while hiking. I also put snowballs in my hands to get used to the cold, and pushed myself to endure the chilling ice. When most people were looking to go up in good weather, I prayed for bad and went up when I knew it was going to be windy, cold, snowing, and miserable (what I figured Everest might be on a good day). I shouted into the wind, laughed, and grinned so much that more than a few times, my face froze in a smile.

It wasn't always great fun, smiles, and a picnic in the park.

After going up Longs Peak a few times, Seth and I decided to hit some more 14,000-foot peaks for additional training and to get back into altitude as often as possible. We did some research and picked Grays and Torreys Peaks. It seemed logical to us because they weren't too far from Estes. Grays is the highest mountain on the Continental Divide, and Torreys is a trough and a ridge away; both can be done in the same day. Not much technical equipment is needed for the normal routes, but we were just getting in shape and building a base of long hours on the mountains.

In early August, we hit the trail at about six A.M. It was an incredibly beautiful day, with the Continental Divide drifting behind us and to our left. Heading up, we passed a couple of people; one had even brought a dog along. (That goes to tell you how technical this peak is, huh?) By the time we made it to the summit of Grays, the clouds were rolling in, and all we could see was white and about fifteen feet in front of us. Think of it as hiking inside a Ping-Pong ball. We managed to befriend a few people on the summit, and one of them wanted to check out Torreys Peak, so we invited him to follow us down into the trough and back up the other side to the next summit.

While resting at the top of the next mountain, eating granola bars and drinking hot water, I noticed how great I felt. I wasn't the least bit tired, and the thinner air felt incredible in my lungs. Eager to get back down, and feeling more than a little brave, we headed off the trail. If you ever get the opportunity to climb Torreys, look to the right and you'll notice the enormous face running directly down from the summit. Not exactly a great thing to come down, especially since it's scree-ridden. Scree is loose rock, and very unstable, because every step down, it slides and takes you with it (much like hiking down a steep sand dune), causing a minor avalanche with a possibility of something much worse.

We decided it would be fun to go down the face of the mountain screeing ("skiing" on scree). The scree turned into a technical climb, and Seth and I had to down-climb using our hands and what little we had taught ourselves at this point in the training. Seth was over to my right, working his way down a large boulder, when all of a sudden he lost his hold and disappeared behind the rock, falling about ten feet. He lost his trekking poles and somehow managed to get his footing back, narrowly avoiding tumbling a couple thousand feet to his death.

Within those microseconds, I had so many thoughts go through my head: What do I do now? How do I get him down? What if he dies? What if he breaks something? What's going to happen? Every scenario blasted through my brain, all in a split second. They say your life flashes before your eyes before you die, but they don't say anything about what flashes before your eyes when it's your little brother's life on the line. I just thank God his life was saved.

From then on out, it was a slow, methodical climb down until we managed to get back on the trail and hike the rest of the way to the car. That was one close call I never want to have happen again. I learned to always check the footing, the route, and head down with caution.

Practically every morning I was up running. Snow, rain, wind, cold, heat, it didn't matter. I had a goal in mind, and I knew I was going to accomplish it, or at least do everything in my power, so that if by chance I didn't make it, it wouldn't be for lack of trying. Every day I'd read more of the mountaineering book, studying it, rereading it, and practicing in my head everything that might happen. I did a lot of visualization and truly saw myself on Everest climbing. I read plenty of books on Everest, the route, the food, the accidents—everything.

Also, while climbing, training, running, and learning as much as I could about mountaineering, I was still in negotiations with companies for sponsorship. Day in, day out, I'd be sitting on my butt, working on the computer, chatting on the phone, making meetings with people, and trying to get things accomplished. I'd try to get at least one item accomplished every single day.

I can't tell you how many times I would get up at six A.M. and work straight through until three A.M. There would be so many times when I'd put a potato in the microwave for lunch and forget about it until it was time for dinner. I was a wreck, but one thing I didn't have to worry so much about was food and money. Seth and I had both saved before we left home, and he supported me as much as he could. We had free housing (obviously, living out of the back of my car and in a tent was free, but the solid foundation was nice), we helped around the Evergreens when we could so we could pay our way and not feel like leeches, and the training was going well.

The only thing that wasn't coming in was the support we needed to make the climb itself. The financial support was nowhere near what I was hoping to get. The exposure and the sponsorships never came, which was a huge problem, since we had under a year to get in touch with some Everest organizers and raise the funding to pay for the trip. I managed to get in front of countless companies who all said they'd help out and support the trek monetarily, but when the speech was over and the dust settled, I was out of sight, out of mind. Most of them never responded to my e-mails, phone calls, smoke signals, whatever.

I felt like I kept banging my head on the side of a brick wall and nothing was happening. I even had a cancer organization steal my idea of putting the first cancer survivor on Everest. They said they wanted to help, thought it was an incredible idea, and were willing to do everything they could. Then one day no phone call back, no e-mail reply, and the president would never answer my phone calls.

For the longest time, I was wondering what had happened, until I did some research on the Internet. I found that the cancer organization had partnered with a company I was talking to. They had developed their own team, gotten a cancer survivor, and were going to try to beat me up the mountain. Obviously, that didn't happen, but in the long run, it made me realize that everyone has his own agenda, and you have to be careful whom you talk to. I also couldn't believe that they didn't understand it wasn't a race—it was about the story, it was about the dream, and it was about helping others.

After talking to companies, begging, pleading, and bothering people so often, our big break finally came.

Earlier in the year, I had filled out some forms for a company and their new marketing plans. Something called "Keep Walking" by Jonnie Walker was sent to me in an overnight package, inviting us to New York City to present our idea to a board and try to get $100,000 of funding. This was it. I knew this was going to work, and I knew we were on the right track again. My fading hope was lifted, and I was raring to get moving on something positive for a change.

While we were in New York, someone thought it would be a good idea to toss a couple of airplanes into some skyscrapers down the road from us on the same day I was supposed to deliver the presentation. September 11, 2001, was a shock to the entire world, and our event was put on hold again. We escaped to Philadelphia and flew back to Denver, safe but a little shaken up.

After much rescheduling and anticipation, we gave a presentation to the group, and they awarded us $25,000. Even with the flag fund-raiser, the random donations, and the support from others, however, we were still going to fall short of funding the trip. I didn't care. I knew we were going to make it there, and I knew I was going to climb Everest. Seth might not be able to make it because we didn't have the funds, but at least he would be at Base Camp with me for support. I was going to head up the mountain. I knew this in my soul, and I still didn't lose hope.

He took things surprisingly well. He'd known that his not climbing was a possibility during the planning phase back on the East Coast. He understood we were possibly on the verge of something big, affecting the world, giving hope and inspiration to people. As well as being the incredibly supportive brother that he is, he did everything he could to be there and continue that support. It sometimes created a lot of stress, because I was training by myself and we got into arguments, but the bottom line was, we supported each other.

Slowly, things started to come into play with sponsors, and we managed to get outfitted by Cabela's and Gore-Tex. It was a dual sponsorship, and some of my worries started to fade, though not all. I knew we still had a long time, but after 9/11, it would be difficult if not impossible to get people to part with their dollars. Not only that, but we didn't have the funding to climb Cho Oyu, and I wouldn't get any high-altitude experience before tackling the Big One.

Another problem was getting the permit and organizing the

expedition. Every single person and company I managed to get in front of said there was no way they were going to take a one-lunged, two-time-cancer-surviving lunatic up the highest mountain in the world. I was also told there was no way I would get past Camp 2 (roughly 21,000 feet). Not only would I have to get a company to believe in me and my ability (by this time I had climbed most of the mountains near my house and taught myself plenty of mountaineering skills), but I also had to convince the American Alpine Club to give me an endorsement letter to climb Everest. Every American who attempts to climb Everest has to get an endorsement letter from the American Alpine Club. That letter is then sent to the Nepalese government to review before the climber's name gets put onto a climbing permit.

So not only did I have to worry about getting the funding, I also had to worry about getting funding for a company that wouldn't take us once we got the funding, which we might never get. I also had to convince the Alpine Club to write that letter, book the flights, train more, get more funding—it was an endless circle. It was like a bad sitcom made worse, because none of this was any laughing matter, at least not to me or Seth or any of the people whose names were on that flag we hoped to pin to the top of the world. Eventually, though, I got in touch with a company in Kathmandu who believed in what I was doing and gave me a chance. I was offered a spot on an expedition they were organizing for National Geographic, and without thinking twice, I took it.

All the working, convincing, calling, and training had sucked every bit of my energy. So much so that when I was out training one spectacular day, we had a little accident.

Seth and I had gone into the mountains to get some glacier

practice with crampons, rescue, and other glacier travel skills. We were having a wonderful time sliding down the glacier on our butts and practicing self-arrest (one of the few ways to stop yourself from sliding off the side of a mountain is to roll over and dig your ice axe into the ice and snow).

After playing on the glacier and having a good time in the sun and snow, we were heading back to the car, hiking on the boulders, rocks, and tremendously uneven ground. Seth was a bit behind me until I lost my footing. In an instant, I was on the ground. On my way down, I had tried to toss my ice axe out of the way, but the head got caught up in some rocks, and the end was sticking up, with the rest of it lodged in between boulders. With my weight and inertia pulling me down to earth at a whopping speed, I landed on my side and directly on the sharp point of the axe. Adrenaline-filled, I immediately pulled it out of my side, right under my armpit. Rolling over, I screamed, "Get the hell over here!"

Seth could see a hole in my side about half an inch deep and about a quarter inch wide. Red meat could be seen through the hole. Blood wasn't pouring out, thank God, and we tried to rush to the car, still about three quarters of a mile away. Every so often I would have to stop and get my head straight because I kept almost passing out from the pain. Each time this happened, Seth took the opportunity to check the gash. His worried face was far from reassuring.

At times I got amazingly cold and had to put on some more clothes. Moving forward, I kept fighting off light-headedness. I was also thinking about what to do and where to go. Seth immediately said I had to go to the hospital, but my insurance company wouldn't allow me a renewal if I filed a claim, so I wanted to keep it for emergencies only. Not little things like, oh, say, meat chunks coming out of your underarm, or passing out every five minutes. You know, just the really big stuff.

I even tried to joke a little about being thirsty and how it would be funny if the water spurted out of the hole in my side like in a cartoon. When we got to the car, Seth drove down and tried to hurry, ignoring my irrational humor, but everyone on the road must have been going five miles per hour that day. Every bump and turn hurt more than the last; I had gone from the relatively pain-free adrenaline rush to the cold and harsh bite of reality. I was dealing with the pain in my head and kept telling myself it was good and I could handle anything. I'm Superman.

While Seth drove, we talked about what to do and where to go. The local clinic was closed. The hospital was too expensive, and our friend who was a nurse lived too far away; we didn't even know if she was there to begin with. Thank God a member of the family upstairs at the Evergreens had worked in the emergency room as a nurse when she was younger. Having her clean out the wound was cute, because her grandkids were trying to help as well. One of them even said, "Sean, I have a rainbow Band-Aid, will that help?"

After the nurse fixed me, I sat up, and everything went distant. People's voices echoed throughout the room, and I felt like I was going to pass out. Fortunately, I didn't; they were able to stabilize me. I took a number of Tylenol, was helped downstairs to lie on the couch, and tried to sleep. Getting up for bed wasn't easy, since I had pierced my muscles, though my ribs had stopped the ice axe from puncturing my lungs. Good Lord, was I lucky.

But at the same time I was thanking my lucky stars, I was upset that this had happened in the first place. All I could think about was how it was going to throw off our schedule for climbing Rainier in Seattle. I decided I was still going to go, and I would be better by the time we headed up to Washington. Believe it or not, I was up and about in a couple of days, never saw a professional doctor (I couldn't afford it), and a month later, Seth and I took off by ourselves for a climb up Rainier.

Rainier. That's an incredible mountain we were using for training and more glacier practice. Normally, people join expedition groups to go up this peak, but Seth and I thought we knew enough about climbing that we could tackle it ourselves. Our goal was to climb to the summit via a route called Disappointment Cleaver, and rightfully so. It was the first mountain I attempted to climb where I didn't reach the summit.

For once I couldn't blame it all on myself. It might have had something to do with the eventful week before we drove to Washington. Not only did we drive all day and night to get there and head up this giant volcano encased in over thirty-five square miles of snow and glacial ice, but a few days prior, I had climbed the highest mountain in Colorado, as well as a few more 14ers (mountains over 14,000 feet) with my pack-o-rocks.

On the day of the unsuccessful attempt at Rainier, we climbed to the first camp (Camp Muir), slept about two hours, and headed out onto the glacier and over to the Cleaver. Heading up and about three quarters of the way into the trip, I had to make an incredibly difficult decision. My body had been tested to the max the week before, and it finally found its limit. I knew I could make it to the summit, but since climbing is a round-trip sport, I wasn't certain I could have a safe trip down.

After Seth and I discussed things, we decided to come down, disappointed. Although it wasn't a success, we were still alive, and I learned a lot from the failure—that it wasn't a failure at all but a learning experience, as most "failures" are. Planning, growing, learning, never putting my life in danger, and understanding that the mountain will always be there; I might not be. Besides, it's a good excuse to visit Seattle again.

With about eight months of climbing under my belt, countless trips up Longs Peak and the other 14ers in Colorado, carrying two hundred pounds of weight in my backpack, my chicken legs were in shape enough for Everest (or so I thought). Only problem was, we still didn't have the funding. I had secured an Everest organizer, convinced the American Alpine Club that I was qualified to climb Everest, and we were a go with everything but the funding. A little funding here, a little there, donations for gear, and we were covered from head to toe with everything we needed. Little did the companies know that we didn't have the funds to get us to the mountain (you might say that's a slight problem).

With the deadline fast approaching, and with the flights booked, we were about a month away from departure, still owing money to the company in Kathmandu. We didn't buy an entire permit to climb ($70,000), but we did manage to wrangle a spot on another one. With no more time left to collect funding, I took every penny of savings I had in the bank—every stock, every bond, everything I owned—and sold it. Every last thing I had was gone. I thought about robbing some banks, but with a brother who stands six feet seven, he might be pretty easy to pick out of a lineup.

Regardless, we were going to Nepal to attempt Everest. What was going to happen when I got back? I had no idea. It was the opposite of our trip up Rainier. Not summiting the volcano had been a conscious decision. Seth and I had played the part of mature, practiced, well-trained climbers who recognized their limits and realized that by busting a nut to get to the top, we might not have any juice left to get back down.

Everest was something completely different. Over the years it had become the ultimate test for endurance athletes everywhere. You trained smart everywhere else just to get to Everest; what happened there was often up to the mountain. Could you adequately train for a beast like Everest? It's debatable, but Seth and I had certainly done our best.

The challenge of climbing the world's tallest mountain is equal parts physical and mental. You climb, make decisions, climb some more, decide again. Every day is a mini–gut check. Do you have the stamina to go on? Can you stomach the temperature, the altitude, the endurance, and the pain?

A lot of people in the climbing world doubted my abilities because I hadn't been tested on some of the highest mountains. I could sympathize with them. Hell, I hadn't even been able to make it up Rainier. But how many expert high-altitude climbers had failed at Everest despite being in excellent physical shape and having years of experience? Plenty, that's how many.

Before a climb like Everest, a man looks in the mirror, literally and figuratively. He asks himself some questions, big ones; he finds the answers deep within. I'd done my soul-searching, my training, my fund-raising, my finagling, my praying. I was ready, and I wasn't going alone. It wasn't a question of endurance or training or money anymore—it was man against mountain, and I would not, could not, fail.

After all, I had a lot of people counting on me.

CHAPTER TEN

THE BLACK MARKET

❖

We had just been delayed for over an hour and were finally taking off. A tire on the airplane had to be replaced, and jokingly, I said to Seth, "I wonder if we'll feel the plane lean to one side when they jack it up." (They actually put it on, then inflated it.)

Our flight schedule was about to take us twelve time zones away from Colorado and halfway around the world. Kathmandu, Nepal, was our destination city. However, getting to the hub of Everest expeditions was about as far from a straight shot as you could get: We flew through two different countries before landing. Denver to Los Angeles to Taipei (Taiwan) to Bangkok (Thailand) to Kathmandu was our schedule through roughly three days of travel.

Saying goodbye to everyone—family, friends, loved ones—was one of the hardest things I've ever had to do, emotionally speaking. I was pretty sure I was coming back, unlike when I drove to Jacksonville with no idea what I was doing. Now I had a clear goal and knew exactly what I was doing. So when I said goodbye to the family at the Evergreens and then my mom and dad (they had flown in to see Seth and me before we left), it was extremely hard.

I cried and couldn't control it, but somewhere deep down I was pretty confident I was coming back, so it softened the blow as much as possible. In a way, I didn't feel as bad as I should have, leaving them behind, because I knew what I had in front of me, and I knew that I had the skills to accomplish my goal. I did feel bad about going halfway across the world without any guarantee for them to hold on to. Knowing they were in pain over my departure made the goodbyes all the more difficult. I can't stand seeing pain in anyone's eyes.

I loved them all dearly, and it tore at my heart knowing they were emotionally distraught because of something I was doing, no matter how worthy the cause. I looked into their eyes and saw worry, doubt, and despair. I wondered later why I'd done this to my real family and my pseudo family (the Evergreens family had become like our own family, and it was almost as hard saying goodbye to them). Then I realized that I was trying to inspire and instill hope in cancer patients and survivors around the globe. God be with me—and them.

Midway through the first leg of our flight, I looked out the window in time to see one of the most beautiful sunsets I'd seen in a long time. It made me realize how lucky I was to be going halfway around the world to climb a mountain and see the most beautiful mountain range on earth. I had been incredibly lucky just to come this far, to be alive and on this flight. Granted, it would be great to summit, but watching that sunset on the plane made me realize I'd be happy to just get on the mountain, let alone reach the top.

I knew how much summitting meant to everybody—my parents, who believed in me; Seth, who'd been there through thick and thin to get us both this far; the cancer patients whose names were on my flag; and most of all myself—but not at the cost of my life (been there, done that). I had way too much ahead of me to risk losing everything I'd worked so hard for. I wanted to come back alive and with experiences to share with others.

I couldn't do that if I was just another Everest statistic.

After the flight from Denver to L.A., we checked in again and were told we would have to get our bags in Bangkok and recheck them before we left for Kathmandu because of security reasons. We'd have a day/night layover and would have to put the bags in airport storage. Then Seth and I would go around Bangkok and look for a safe hotel to rest and phone home. It promised to be an interesting flight, since it was about fifteen hours.

I was pretty nervous about the trip and what was going to happen, but I knew once we got to Kathmandu and we were with Wongchu (the organizer), everything would be okay. Then again, it was a challenge—it was an adventure. And I might not ever get this chance again. I needed to relax and enjoy the trip.

Good luck relaxing: We were supposed to board at eleven, but we were informed it wouldn't be until eleven-forty because of the late arrival of our new plane. Even though we were in L.A., every announcement coming over the airport speakers was in four different languages, with English last. Weren't we still in the United States? I guess because we were headed overseas to a distant land, everyone else needed to know what was going on first. Figures! I'm always the last to know.

I was also pretty tired, since it was by now twelve-twenty A.M. on my body time (Colorado time), and the last three or four days of training had been incredibly draining. My life wouldn't be my life unless it was hard. Then again, someone had told me once that nothing worth doing comes easy.

This trip had promised to be an adventure and had already

turned into one. Everyone was running around speaking Chinese and Taiwanese. I was still just trying to figure out the time zone thing. At last we left LAX, bound for Bangkok, at midnight. That would be Wednesday the twentieth. We passed through the time zones and the international date line, making it the twenty-first. Okay, so say it was six A.M. when we were passing the international date line. Does it become six A.M. the next day? I thought so but wasn't sure. Just one more surreal aspect to an already *Twilight Zone*–like trip.

What's worse, I was crammed into a middle seat on the fifteen-hour flight and was none too happy about it. I'm six feet two. I could only imagine how Seth felt. I could have moved to another seat but would have been forty-some rows away from Seth. In the end, I should have done it, because it would have been nice to sleep in an aisle seat or exit row.

A little later, we were in the air, the same place we'd been since about twelve-forty-five L.A. time. It was now seven-forty-five, so I'd been in the air, packed in like a sardine, for roughly seven hours. The best part was I still had about six more to go; our ETA around six. So far we'd been treated really well. Everything had been great except for the shots of juice they gave us. Yeah, the juice might be enough for a two-year-old, because they served about two ounces and no more. Maybe that was enough for most people who flew EVA Air, but for Americans used to supersizing, that didn't cut it.

The food, on the other hand, was really good. It started off with a package of rice cakes covered with peanuts and peas. After that, we had a choice of fish or chicken. I chose chicken, since I don't like fish too much. There was also a small salad, some fruit, and a funky-looking molded Jell-O-type food that had a hint of butterscotch with the consistency of really soft pudding. I didn't eat it. One bite and . . . nah. Oh, and then the shot of O.J.

In between sampling new and inventive Asian cuisine, I'd been trying to sleep by listening to Channel 5 on the plane, the classical channel. They had a couple of movies playing and served Cup O' Soup during the shows, with a shot of apple juice this time. I think I may have felt something on my parched palate. They also had different radio stations to play with. The Beatles were playing on one, some funky Chinese techno on another one, and random other things, I'm not even sure what they were.

Announcements hadn't been made in a while, and I was wondering where we were en route. I knew we were flying over the Pacific, but where? Were we about halfway there? Or was there longer still to fly? At least the mundane details of the trip were a distraction from the ordeal I'd be facing once we returned to terra firma. According to the computer-generated map showing our location, we should have passed Hawaii and been under the Bering Straits. I was listening to "The Barber of Seville" for the third time on trusty Channel 5. You would think that with such a long flight, they'd have longer or more songs so they didn't repeat as often. Now it was time to try to relax and sleep in this sardine can they called a plane. My seat was no wider than my shoulders. Also, about five sixths of the people were Asian, and Seth and I stuck out like sore thumbs. I told myself we'd better get used to it, because we were about to be guests in a country where most people didn't speak English and were much shorter than I was used to.

It was now 12:01 on March 21, 2002, Taipei time. I was watching *Behind Enemy Lines* and doubting my ability to climb Everest. I'd been feeling great a while back, but suddenly, I was having second thoughts about this adventure. I knew if I didn't do it now, someone else would. I was wondering if it was worth my life. I knew I'd be helping people, and I also knew I could be an inspiration to many. I just couldn't let any negative thoughts enter my head. It was going to be a long haul, and I was excited to get everything done with and to get it under way. I kept telling myself, *Positive thoughts only. Recognize the negative, but don't dwell there. Only positive thoughts. I can do this, and I know I will. I will summit and return safely from Everest and continue to help others.*

After a pretty short, uneventful layover in Taipei, Taiwan (where two locals wanted my brother and me to stay with them so they could give us a Thai massage), we made it to Bangkok. It was Friday, March 22. We were at the Bangkok airport, checking in and on our way to Kathmandu—almost. When the airline representative at the counter asked for our passports, Seth reached for his but produced nothing.

He couldn't remember where he'd seen it last, and he also couldn't remember seeing it fall out. I think what happened was that we checked through customs at the Bangkok airport, and he haphazardly put it into his regular pocket, not taking the extra time to put it into his buttoned, more secure pocket. When we got into the tuk-tuk (a three-wheeled, small-motored taxi), it fell out in the street, or it was left in the hotel and the cleaning lady picked it up. Quite possibly it was pulled out of his pocket and sold on the black market. Apparently, passports go for a huge amount of money in Thailand; however, I don't know too many Thai people who are his height. Either way, when we went to get our boarding passes to fly to Kathmandu, he didn't have his passport.

Let me back up. At the Bangkok baggage claim the day earlier, we'd had one bag come out. So while Seth and I were waiting for the other bags, I went to the airline counter. They couldn't understand how I'd gotten a bag, so I tried telling them I had to get them all and recheck. "No," they said very firmly, and security took the one bag and checked it through. As far as I could see, my bag had just disappeared again.

Next we went to a sign that said TOURIST INFORMATION. "Tourist information no here," the guy behind the counter said to us. Huh? Instead of trying to figure that one out, we went to the taxi. Later, we checked in to a hotel room that the taxi driver suggested, had a short tour of Bangkok, and fell asleep, exhausted.

After we ate breakfast, the same taxi driver who had taken us to the hotel took us back to the airport. Then Seth couldn't find his passport. So instead of being on my way to Nepal, I was sitting in the American embassy in Bangkok, where I met a guy who had bought black bills. These were supposedly hundred-dollar bills covered in some kind of a black material. Apparently, when washed, the material would come off, and the bill would look normal. I couldn't help but roll my eyes, knowing how much of a scam that was. He had gotten drunk the night before, and some Aussie leaving the country sold him eight hundred-dollar bills for two hundred. A chemical was supposed to wash them clean. He was hoping they'd work. I was doubting it would.

Eventually I used the pay phone outside the embassy. After talking to the Thai Airlines people, who spoke very broken English, I rebooked the flight for the following day and took care of the luggage (in airport storage). Next I got in contact with a Mr. Gonzalez, who worked at the embassy. He was a great help. I talked to him about what we were doing, why we were there, and where we were going. He and the U.S. embassy expedited Seth's passport so we could get it that day and not a week or so later. He also helped by e-mailing the group in Kathmandu. We got a confirmation e-mail back, and all was okay. Funny how dependent we are on other people in a foreign land, out of our comfort zone.

We waited till about two-forty-five for Seth to get his new passport, then we went to Thai immigration, then to the airport hotel for another night in Bangkok. We'd get a room and then fly to Kathmandu the next day and take care of everything. We were cutting this all very close. We were supposed to start trekking to Base Camp on Sunday. I could only hope we'd make it.

After we got to the airport, Seth watched our carry-on luggage while I went to the reservations desk to see what was going on with our flights and checked bags. Broken English from the lady behind the counter told me, I think, "Tomorrow, ten-thirty, flight 319." I sure hoped I'd understood that correctly. I left a message with Mr. Gonzalez at the U.S. embassy to send our Kathmandu group an e-mail telling them what flight and when. OK, now we can go back to our flight to Kathmandu.

Flying into Nepal, I saw my first view of Mount Everest. It was spectacular. It was eye level with the plane, and the mountains were so far away. It was absolutely unbelievable. I couldn't imagine standing on top of something I was seeing—at eye level—from my seat on a passenger jet. The thought of summiting became very real. My stomach dropped.

At the Kathmandu airport, we got in line to get a permit and to pay for our visas. We went downstairs, x-rayed our carry-on bags, and then went to get our checked bags. Think they were there? After all the hassle we had in L.A., the miscommunication in Bangkok, and the one bag we did have eventually disappearing behind closed doors? Nope. Figures, right?

We went to the Kathmandu baggage claim to report our luggage as missing. Pemba, one of the guys from the Kathmandu expedition (the local folks we were meeting and climbing with), came up to help us. He was a native of the area, and he told the guy in charge of the baggage claim what was going on and what we thought had happened. Thai Airlines had told me the day before (in Bangkok after the passport incident) and the day before that (in Bangkok the day we arrived there) that they had my bags and had held them in security until yesterday (the day we were to leave Bangkok). Yeah, sure. The truth of the matter was that our luggage was on the flight we were *supposed* to be on but *couldn't* get on because Seth didn't have his passport. The baggage claim people got our bags in Kathmandu and put them in storage when they arrived. Moral of the story—don't believe anyone. Just have faith that your stuff will make it somewhere.

Finally, lying in bed at the Tibet Guest House later that day, I was again questioning my ability to do the expedition. I was probably the most inexperienced person to ever climb Everest. Somehow, that scary statistic didn't bother me as much as it probably should have. In my head, I knew I was going to do fine. I had faith that this was what I was supposed to do. I kissed my necklace every once in a while. My grandma had given me a religious charm when I was battling cancer. It went into storage after I went into remission the second time, but I pulled it back out and put it around my neck when I arrived in Kathmandu.

I was still confident and anxious to get going; however, uncertainty crept into my head when I saw other people I thought were climbers. I got nervous, but I pushed it away because I was doing this for myself and others touched by cancer, not the other climbers. Either way, I *would* get up this mountain. Besides, my journey was about *being* there, dream chasing, and living. Not being scared to take chances.

Speaking of chances, the phone rang just then.

"Hello?" I answered, wondering what calamity might befall Seth and me next.

"Yes, are you with Peak Promotions?" came a lilting voice from the other end of the phone. Definitely un-calamity-like.

"Yes, who is this?"

"Jeevan Schrestha. I'm with Miss Hawley." Damn, she *was* good. And wow, did they move fast! Miss Hawley was *the* mountaineering correspondent for Everest and other mountains in Nepal and throughout the Himalayas. She worked with the Reuters News Agency, *American Alpine Journal, Himalayan Journal* (India), *Alp* (Italy), *Climber* (U.K.), *Desnivel* (Spain), *Die Alpin* (Switzerland), *Vertical* (France), and *Yama-Kei* (Japan).

I had no idea how she'd heard about the expedition, but every bit of news coverage I could get was incredible. That would mean my story was going to get to more people. This expedition wasn't about me doing something for me, it was about me doing something for people touched by cancer. It held a higher purpose: hope.

After the short meeting with the Himalayan master herself, Seth, Pemba, and I went to meet with Wongchu, who ran the local expedition company. We discussed everything we had to take care of and what we needed, from radios to granola bars to ice axes to boots. We also met the guys who would be on the expedition team, and the true climbers of the group—the Sherpa guides. All three (two climbers, one cook) seemed pretty nice. They said they felt comfortable with me and were happy to see I was in good shape. They'd been worried because I'd had cancer, and in Nepal, there was no such thing as a cancer survivor.

After the meeting, Seth and I walked around Kathmandu and took in the sights. Despite its romantic and literary heritage, the city is a very old and dirty place with garbage shoved into the alleys and little kids selling pot. The buildings are shoved together like stained, crooked teeth, and the roads are congested with not only people but cars, bikes, and motorcycles.

Since there are no sidewalks on many of the streets, it's a wonder more people don't get hit by the motorcycles darting in and out of human traffic. Amid the labyrinth of confusing streets and past the congestion lies the history of the city and the habitants' religious beliefs and incredible faith. While walking through the city, we saw a little girl who is the goddess of good trips. People don't see her very often, so it was incredibly good luck that we managed to catch a glimpse of this living deity through a window in her home. On the way back to the hotel, I also knelt at a little shrine covered with prayer flags, silk scarves, and painted idols and got blessed in front of Ganish, the god of safe travels and good fortune.

Back at the hotel, we met with Wongchu and the Sherpas again. He and Nima Gombu (a seven-time Everest summiter and one of my Sherpas) went through the equipment, seeing what I needed. Everything was great, except I didn't have a Himalayan suit. Translation: I didn't have what was basically a huge sleeping bag with a hood, legs, and arms. (Think the younger brother's snowsuit in *A Christmas Story,* just a little bigger.) Sounds like science fiction, maybe, but it could be a big problem when the temperature dipped to minus-40.

We went to some of Wongchu's friends in town, and I got measured for a suit. If I couldn't get one shipped over from the States, Wongchu would have one made for me. The last thing I wanted to do, since this expedition was on a shoelace budget (make that a shoeless budget, since we didn't even have shoes to put the laces in), was to have someone make me a custom down suit.

Despite the good news/bad news scenario, I had a great night's sleep. When I woke up the next morning, I headed out to see if I could start doing something right with my life. One of the main reasons for climbing Everest was to inspire others touched by cancer and give them some hope for the future.

There was a local hospital called the Bhaktapur Cancer Care Center where I wanted to talk to the patients, the parents, the doctors, and the nurses. It was something I wasn't sure I could emotionally handle, but I had brought something from Colorado I was going to give a patient at that hospital, so we headed over to see if I could offer some hope.

It hardly looked like a hospital when we pulled into the parking lot. I saw the operating rooms, the doctors' scrubs, the masks, the gloves, but this was more like an infirmary, somewhere kids would go in school if they had a fever or cold.

My fair skin, height, and hiking clothes had made a swift and obvious impression, and I felt conspicuous in my health. I also felt guilty, as I sometimes do when I visit hospitals. I had won my battle; they might not. I was instantly reminded of my mortality in a way I hadn't been in years.

Inside, the impression was little better. The posters on the wall—those feel-good ones doctors always plaster everywhere to cover up the death and decay—were outdated and curling at the edges, just like the celery-green paint that covered the cinder-block walls. The office with one desk was home base for about four or five different doctors. After I met with them, told them my story, and shared my ideas about hope and inspiration, they understood what I was trying to do and agreed to a tour and patient interaction.

The rooms, about four of them, held the children, adults, and families. These were the saddest rooms in the building, the loneliest, and by far the scariest. Ten beds lined the walls of the room where we stood, an impromptu assembly of doctors, nurses, my brother, me, and some very, very sick patients.

The beds were separated by a thin, sagging curtain. Though a doctor told us that most of the children were too sick to get out of bed, he was being redundant; their hollow, tired eyes told me all I needed to know. But the concrete walls and depressing drapes couldn't dim the enthusiasm of the doctors here. Their energy was spontaneous; even with the past dredging up in my innards, I could hardly help but be amazed at their sheer audacity in the face of such crippling pain. The director, a portly gentleman with thinning hair, addressed the patients personally, his voice infectious, his hands gesticulating wildly as he spoke rapidly in the garbled beauty of Nepalese.

My tour guide extraordinaire and de facto interpreter explained in whispered tones that the director was telling my story; that's why he was so animated. At one point my tour guide stood on the toes of his worn sneakers to deliver the director's final salvo: "This man is a survivor—and you will be, too! He is leaving tomorrow to climb Mount Everest!"

A ripple passed across their faces: I recognized it as the glimmer of hope I had felt with each passing day of survival. Here I was, imagining these kids to be my reflection, but they were seeing in me what they yearned to see in themselves. God, how I recognized that look. I saw hope in their eyes that bubbled through the chemo, defying the bone weariness and nausea to rise to the surface and spread across taut, weary faces. Eyes long dead lit up, and fingers long curled rose to give the universal thumbs-up of Fonzie-like approval.

Remember the T-shirt my dad got for me so I didn't feel like the outcast? So I wouldn't have to explain to people why I looked as I did? Why I was sixty pounds overweight, bald, and as pale as a full moon? My dad gave that shirt to me, and it brought me good luck. Here I was, fourteen years later, standing at the foot of the world's tallest mountain in a cancer hospital where children climbed their own personal Everests every single day. With the director of the hospital serving as my interpreter, I strode from bed to bed, hugging the patients, taking photos, and gently patting bald heads, creating ear-to-ear smiles.

I had brought the shirt from home as a symbol of good luck and hope. As I was standing in front of a bed in which a pale teenager lay, his head free of hair and his eyes full of life, I knew he was the one. His face was renewed with enthusiasm, his thin body straining against his pasty-white sheets to rise and shake my hand. It also happened that he was battling Hodgkin's disease and was in the fourth stage. He was also thirteen years old.

Halfway across the world, but he was just like me.

I reached for my pack, then whispered a short message to the director as I grabbed my lucky shirt and pulled it free of the protein bars and long underwear. It vibrated in my trembling hands, a living thing, a thin, worn piece of material that held more emotional worth than all of my donations combined.

It was a simple shirt, really, a homemade affair of green material and white lettering, a typical 1980s T-shirt. The front read I DON'T ALWAYS LOOK LIKE THIS; the back let people know I'M ON CHEMO. God, how often that shirt had comforted me through nights spent racked over the toilet or sweating bullets in my bed. Many was the endless night in which I thought I'd be buried in that shirt. I swallowed the thought and looked at the boy; it was like looking in a mirror. How strange to think you can come halfway around the world to stare at yourself.

The director translated the words as I handed it to the boy, who quickly grabbed it up and pulled it on. The director told the young boy and the people in the room that the shirt was a symbol of hope and good luck.

I told the patient that when he got better and his cancer was gone, he had to pass the shirt on to another young child battling cancer. The shirt had helped me, so he knew it would help him as well.

I nodded approvingly at the boy, staring at the shirt I'd been too sick to wear on too many occasions, though it had always brought me luck nonetheless. Around him, the other children perked up, staring at the boy and his new shirt as he translated its meaning to one and all.

It was indeed a magical shirt, as I soon found out about a year later, when I was giving a presentation that the doctor from the Bhaktapur Cancer Care Center attended. He came up to me after the talk to let me know that not only did the shirt help the young patient recover from cancer, but it was on the back of a fourth survivor.

It was time to go. The children were clearly tired, though at least now most of their faces held a weary smile. Though I could no longer see many of their sleeping eyes, I hoped my visit had meant even a fraction as much to them as it had meant to me. I turned from the hospital and stared from the bottom of the Kathmandu Valley up to where I knew the world's tallest mountain jolted out of the earth's crust.

Tomorrow I would leave Kathmandu to begin the two-week trek to Base Camp.

Like the children, I would need my rest.

CHAPTER ELEVEN

EVEREST JITTERS

❖

Finally, we were heading to the Kathmandu airport for our long-awaited journey to Everest Base Camp. Walking into the dingy, dirty check-in, we had to put all of our bags through the X-ray machine. I wasn't sure what they were looking for, since everything we were taking up there could have been used as a weapon of some kind, from ice axes to crampons (metal spikes attached to the bottoms of boots to bite into the ice) to highly explosive fuel canisters.

After we went through the motions of airport security, everything was weighed—our checked luggage, our carry-on bags, even us. They had to make sure the plane wasn't overloaded with weight and we could get into Lukla safely. Security was a joke. It looked like an old voting booth. You know the kind, with the drawback curtains and the flimsy wooden two-by-two slats holding it up into a small box. Inside was a security guard asking questions: "Do you have any lighters? Do you have any guns? Do you have any knives?" That was it. I could have lied about everything and had a bazooka in my pants, and they never would have known. I've seen more damage done with an improperly used ice axe or crampon than I ever have with a properly used knife, but that's just me. (Speaking of which, I have a nice scar on my right side below my armpit from the axe incident, so I know firsthand what damage that thing can do.)

The tiny propeller plane sat about twenty people, tops. We had to bend over to walk inside and crawl to our seats like turtles strapped in shells. Two seats on the left side, one on the right, and the aisle working its way from the open pilots' cabin toward the back of the plane, where we boarded. With the curtain separating the cabin from the cockpit open, we could see where we were going and have a close view of the sky in front of us.

After an incredibly choppy takeoff, a few bounces on the tires and a bump into the air, we were airborne. (Gulp!) Of all the challenges I faced climbing Everest, it was the little unexpected things that caused us the most anxiety. A lost passport here, sleepless nights there, shoddy security, and an even shoddier liftoff. Sometimes I thought climbing the Big One would be easier.

Of course, that was before I got a good look at her. From the window, I could see Kathmandu slowly disappearing out of sight and the mountains to my left getting big, bigger, and then biggest. In the distance, I could begin to see the outline of some peaks and their tremendous size.

It's nearly impossible to describe the Himalaya Mountains and do them justice. I could say they were like the Rocky Mountains on steroids, but that still wouldn't do a decent job. The mountains I trained on were like tiny speed bumps compared to these magical giants. As I scanned the horizon and the peaks jutting up higher than our flying altitude, my eyes were drawn toward a mountain in the background.

When I saw her, I knew, not thought, I *knew* it was her.

Everest.

It was almost like she was looking right at me, talking, saying, "I'm here," and letting me know everything was going to be okay.

I whispered under my breath, asking if I could have the strength, good weather, and luck needed to summit. I knew that my youth, vitality, and training weren't enough to reach the top. It would take all that and more; the conditions, the weather, the stamina, the energy would all have to align just so, or I wouldn't make it.

So I held a conversation with her—with Everest—talking to myself, grateful at last for the vibrating shell of the tiny plane and the rumbling of the noisy engines. I was in my own world, looking out and up through the window at a mountain notorious for being not only the highest in the world but also one of the most dangerous.

I closed my eyes and visualized myself on the top, as I had done countless times during all my training in Colorado. I would always see myself on the summit and work backward to see how I had to get there. It was like solving a mystery by knowing whodunit on the last page and backtracking to page one. The feelings were there, the emotions were there; I was already successful. In my eyes, I was already on top, and there was no question about if—only when.

As soon as I was done climbing Everest in my head, we were on our descent and getting ready to land in real time. I noticed the landing strip through the cockpit curtains. At one end were the Himalaya Mountains; at the other end was a cliff. Needless to say, if we went too fast, we'd smack into the mountains and blow up, but if we didn't have the juice to make it all the way onto the runway, we'd hit the cliff where the pavement ran off to the edge. Again, we'd probably blow up.

It was your classic Himalayan win/win scenario.

It also made us feel incredibly safe when we looked out the windows and saw old fuselages lying at the bottom of the cliff.

The landing strip was set at a slight upward angle to stop planes more quickly upon landing and help them accelerate faster on takeoff. The instant we touched ground, our brakes were engaged, and every person in the plane lunged forward from the force. It was a scene straight out of one of those hokey *Airport* movies from the 1970s. I figured if I could make it this far, I'd be pretty good on the near-disaster scale and have a nice chance of making it to the summit, cosmic karma being what it is and all.

After landing, we went inside the terminal building to claim our luggage. With our luck so far, do you think it all got there? Nope. Not a chance. Two of our four bags got there. How can someone lose luggage on a direct flight with only fifteen people on board? Later, I would find out that our plane was overweight at departure and that the luggage was coming on the next day's flight. *Good Lord*, I thought, *I hope so*. We'd already had so many problems, and this certainly wasn't helping.

We hired a couple of porters, "rented" a zup-yak (a female yak) to haul our luggage up to Base Camp, and hit the road. Er, I mean trail. There are no roads up there, just dirt trails. Walking slowly up from Lukla to Phakding (pronounced "pack ding") was our first trip along the nonexistent Himalayan highway system. Lukla was at about 9,000 feet, and we were heading up just a little higher. We slept in a small lodge in Phakding before heading up to 12,500 feet and a village called Namche Bazaar.

As with most of the scenery we were to see on that trip, the hike from Phakding to Namche was stunning. There are steep trails all along the "Everest River" and plenty of bridge crossings to amplify the already heightened pucker factor. Some of the bridges are hundreds of feet above the water and look like they've been around since the first Everest summit in 1953.

In Nepal, the religious feelings are incredibly strong and part of daily life. One tradition is for the local people to present silk scarves blessed by a lama to climbers departing for a trip or expedition. We had plenty of these placed over our heads and around our necks when approaching these bridges. They were supposed to protect us and give us good luck. The scarves also protected the bridges, and the more scarves they saw (i.e., the more people crossing), the more it needed protecting—kind of like a karmic catch-22.

One bridge in particular, just below Namche, had countless silk scarves and prayer flags protecting it and those crossing it. Halfway across, I tied one of my katas (silk scarves) around the bridge handrail. It was very close to my heart, and even now, as I look back, a piece of me prays for everyone crossing that bridge.

Moments like that filled the trip, and after only a few hours in the Himalayas, I was struck by how everything—even the tiniest moments—took on a nearly mystical flavor, a hint of cosmic cumin. When the backdrop is so severe, the trail so rocky, elevated, and challenging, when the wood and the ropes of the bridges you cross are so fragile and ancient, when every step might be your last, life takes on new meaning, and moments stretch to a nearly blissful string of life experiences one can never forget.

Here we'd rest for two nights, and I'd have my first real one-on-one with Everest. I hiked up above the military installation (a Nepalese governmental building to protect locals from the uprising Maoists) to about 13,000 feet, above the village of Namche, which was situated in a large horseshoe-shaped canyon. Namche was carved out in large steps where people built houses, lodges, and small shops. There were even a few bars and restaurants and, incredibly, a pool table.

This village was truly unbelievable because of the resources they had available for us. Satellite Internet for our dispatches to the website, so everyone in the outside world knew what was going on and how we were doing. I also received an e-mail informing me that I had a summit suit being sent from the States by one of our sponsors, so I could rest easier knowing I would have a down suit to wear for the summit push. Prices in town weren't exactly friendly, but anything we needed or wanted, we could find, or it would find us through the Sherpa grapevine, as we'd soon find out in Base Camp.

Approaching the ridge above the military station, I could see Everest's summit, about forty miles in the distance. I ran higher and higher to see her, to get a closer, better view. I managed to sit down on a rock outcropping and get the best view I could possibly find. It was just Everest and me.

For the longest time, I sat there staring, with the mountain looking back at me. It was an incredibly emotional time, and I was flooded with countless thoughts. At one time I started to tear up because I was thinking about this entire trip, this entire thing, this dream I had. There I was, halfway around the world, on my way to attempt to climb to the top of the highest mountain in the world with the hopes, dreams, and prayers of countless people touched by cancer riding on my shoulders. I wanted to get to the summit; I wanted to get them to the summit. I wanted to reach out and into the hearts of everyone touched by cancer to give them hope, to let them know *anything* is possible. A few tears rolled down my cheeks, I murmured some prayers, said, "I'll see you soon" to the mountain, and headed back down to the village.

Later that night, the local cook and two Sherpa guides who would stay at Base Camp with Seth and me played a few hands of the card game Old Maid with us. We had a fantastic time before going to bed. The night was great until I heard a couple of rifle shots around midnight. All through the hike up, we were told to be careful because of the Maoist invasion and the threats of being kidnapped. Apparently, the shots were warning shots to the Maoists, letting them know the Nepali guards were keeping an eye on them and protecting Namche from the Communist group. As if I didn't have enough to worry about.

Because we had two nights in Namche Bazaar, our rest day was actually a short hike to another town and back before another night in town. After waking up early because my nose wouldn't stop dripping, I walked around town until breakfast. Then we all packed up and headed higher into the mountains and closer to Everest.

Kumjung was the next stop, as was the Everest Bakery, at roughly 13,000 feet. I believe this is the highest bakery in the world. Here, it was like an oven. There were no clouds in the sky, no wind, and the radiation of the sun was pounding the building where we were to stay that night.

Before sleeping, we had a conversation with a number of Germans who had heard about the CancerClimber heading to Everest and wanted to take my photo with the Sherpas. It was a snapshot moment for them but an epiphany for me. I remember thinking, *I really hope I can live up to everyone's expectations. I'm going to try my best, and I guess that's all I can do.*

The next stop was Deboche and the Ama Dablam Guest House. I'd heard this place was where *The Hobbit* was set, and I could definitely see how that was possible, with the rhododendron forest blanketing the trail and covering the mountainside. It was about as secluded as one might get and easily could have hidden a race of half-pint halflings, if I didn't know better. We spent a night there, and then we were headed to Dingboche, but not before hearing on the radio that Maoists were in Kathmandu, bombing bridges and killing civilians.

As if we hadn't been through enough—international intrigue, foreign embassies, missing documents, sacked luggage, shaky flights—now kidnapping and possibly death at 13,000 feet? Where was Robert Ludlum when you needed him?

Walking through parts of the Himalayan range was absolutely incredible. Life-changing, even. Sections of the hike were actually flat at about 14,000 feet. It was unbelievable to be walking around and seeing mountains tower over where I was walking. The huge plateau was absolutely mind-boggling. Very spiritual, to say the least.

I think it's impossible to visit Nepal and come back the same person you were when you left. One thing I learned was that life is life. There is no real need for jealousy or greed. It was great knowing I was okay in the middle of nowhere and could manage anywhere. All someone really needs to make it is faith, a smile, and some fun.

Too many people in the U.S. are wrapped up in making money and trying to get ahead of someone else, usually at the other person's expense. It's ridiculous not to live happily with what you have, enjoying the fact that you have that day and your health. I think too many people take that for granted. I realized in the Himalayas, yet again, how lucky I was to be alive. I think everyone should take into consideration how lucky they truly are. This place, this trek, was a reminder of that for me. And if you take me at my word, just think: You can get all this enlightenment without summiting Everest yourself!

More than a few days into the trek to Base Camp, I thought it was time to take a "shower." A shower consisted of a bowl of hot water, some soap, and a cup. The cup was to get my hair wet so I didn't have to shove my head into the bowl. Either way, at nearly 15,000 feet and with snow all around, it was a pretty chilling experience, if you'll forgive the pun. But at least no one could complain about my stinky feet anymore.

Most of the way up to Base Camp, I was being my usual self and having fun with everything. I was living in the moment, the present, enjoying what I had and what was around me. I figured that if I kept building on my small successes, it would help me in the long run with confidence and my mental state. I've found over time that when I'm scared or nervous, I can't function like I can in the present. I was slowly learning how to enjoy the moment again.

I think that when I moved to Jacksonville, I was so concerned about my future and so worried about what I was going to do, I lost myself to having fun in the present. There's a big difference between worrying about the future—having genuine concern so that we do what we need to do each day—and being wrapped up in the future. I was so wrapped up in it, it was ridiculous, and I lost sight of my life.

I also got worried about what others thought, and that was the exact opposite of how I used to be. I thought it was because the people I first associated with were so materialistic, it was unbelievable. I got caught up in the wrong crowd and did some things I regret doing. I've learned now, and I'm still learning, about life and how things work. I believe it's a lifelong process.

There was a fellow in the Kathmandu airport who gave me a Buddhist prayer necklace. We were discussing life and my motto or philosophy. I told him that I lived by five L's—live, love, laugh, learn, and lead by example. Those five things are, I believe, the basis of life. There may be more, if you catch me a few years down the road, I might be up to six or seven L's—but until someone tells me different or I experience it for myself, those are the five L's in my life.

The guy with the necklace actually wrote down the five L's. I found it incredibly interesting, seeing how intrigued he was by what I was doing, and in many ways that was the moment that made me decide to write this book. Next time, I figured, instead of his writing them down, I could just trade him my book for the prayer necklace. Fair swap, right? But I'm glad I could have some influence on his life, and if it helped, then I'm happy.

Through a number of villages and a few hard spots (like horrible sleep, bad dreams, and poor nutrition), we managed to stumble into a town at nearly 17,000 feet. Already, this village was higher than I had ever been on any mountain back in the States. The highest peak I had been on prior to heading to Nepal was the highest peak in Colorado, at about 14,500 feet. Half the size of Everest.

The next morning I woke up and headed to breakfast in the small common room. The trusty Sherpas, Nima Gombu and Pemba (a Sherpa heading to Base Camp with us), were both there, beside what Seth and I had taken to calling "the crap stove" (up this high, there was no wood, so the locals burned dried yak dung). It was warm and smelled of wonderful burning yak patties.

My last meal before heading to Base Camp was breakfast: porridge that I swear was eight years old, because it smelled like old socks. Then I got a one-egg omelet and toast to make a sandwich.

While I was writing in my journal that morning, it was so cold that my pen froze and I had to stick it between my legs to warm it up again. After breakfast, the whole group headed onto the Khumbu Glacier and up to Base Camp.

I had a lot of time to think on the two-week trek to Base Camp and, as was my nature at such times, I had a number of things pass through my head. I focused on having fun while thinking a lot about the people touched by cancer for whom I was doing all this. Also, why—who I was affecting—what I could do by helping people—how I could affect others.

I really needed to concentrate on smiling, having fun, pushing myself, and keeping in mind all the people I was trying to touch. If I made it, I made it. If not, I was still following my dream and trying to prove a point. The point being: Life is finite. Do what you can now. Try to live life before you end up dying, wishing all the while you would have tried something, anything. Take chances and always remember that overcoming fear gives you confidence to try something else. Remain focused no matter what others may say.

And with that in mind, on April 8, we walked into what would be our home for the next month or so. Everest Base Camp. Altitude 17,600 feet. I thought that night, with all the excitement mounting for the events that lay ahead, I'd be waking up every hour or so, but I just tossed a little. I did wake up once and think it had to be about eleven P.M., and wish it were at least that, but as it turned out, I was wrong. Way wrong. It was already four-thirty A.M.! I had an incredible night's sleep.

When I opened the vestibule of the tent, the sun was hitting magnificent peaks to the south of me. It was another beautiful sight in a growing catalog of such moments to behold. That night a couple of avalanches fell. Seracs (large chunks of ice) also came from the icefall region just outside Base Camp.

I knew we were safe there because we were far enough away, but it's still a little unsettling to hear things like that and wonder what might come crashing through your tent at any moment. Back home in the United States, the typical bogeymen were robbers and killers and punks and thieves; here, they were landing-strip cliffs and Maoist kidnappers and avalanches.

Base Camp is on the Khumbu Glacier, nearly rock-covered, except for the huge areas of exposed ice jutting out like small mountains, and constantly changing. The first night I heard rocks tumbling down small cliffs. I hoped that one wasn't headed toward my tent and, eventually, into me. I had a dream about sleeping in my helmet. Each time an avalanche happened, it was like an airplane booming by, like a passenger jet flying overhead.

Before climbing Everest, it's necessary to get permission from the mountain and required by law to have what is called a *puja* ceremony, where a lama chants and talks to the mountain. They believe the mountain is a living goddess called Chomolungma (Mother Goddess of the Earth) and that only those allowed to climb will be worthy of making the summit.

The first thing that went through my mind when I heard this was: *What if I survived cancer, trained for months, moved heaven and earth to get funding, and then came from twelve time zones away and don't get permission to climb the mountain?*

I thought it was a legitimate question and asked one of the Sherpas if that was possible. He replied quite simply, "Yes." Only later did I find out that if we got a negative answer from the

mountain, we were to get another lama, perform another ceremony, and pay that lama more money. Seems like money talks
everywhere in the world, huh?

Sometime before the *puja,* our satellite phone arrived in a fuel
box. We managed to get that working and called home for the
first time in a couple of weeks. The phone call consisted mainly of
my parents crying and me trying to tell them everything was
going to be okay. (Which, as we all know, is universal kid-speak
for "I have no idea what I'm doing here, but it's too late to back
out now, and I'm too old to say 'I want my mommy.' ")

Mom, being the loving person she is, kept saying she was
praying for me. Dad basically said to have fun and enjoy the trip
but also come back alive. I told them not to worry and said we'd
be in touch on a regular basis. If I said my eyes didn't water, I'd be
lying. It was an incredibly emotional conversation.

The second night at Base Camp was great. I woke up only to
go to the bathroom and not due to other things, like moving gla-
ciers, avalanches, kidnappers, revolutionaries, or rock slides. I
did hear a couple of falling seracs that night, though, which made
me wonder how the glacier decides who makes it through and
who doesn't. It was also incredibly cold, and I had to warm my
hands before I continued writing in my journal. My middle finger
on my right hand always got cold. If I was worried about anything
on my trip, it was *that* falling off.

Before heading up into the Khumbu Icefall, we had a day on
the glacier to play around with ice climbing. I say "play," but it
sure didn't make me feel too good when, on our way out, we
heard a fellow climber snap his leg. Again, all this just made me
think: *Who makes it and who doesn't? What if that had been me? Who,
or what, decides?*

The next day we were heading up through the Khumbu Ice-fall—one of the most dangerous sections on the climb—and one we'd have to do about ten times total before the expedition was complete. To climb Everest, expedition members have to accli-mate their bodies to the thin air and altitude by going up and down the mountain numerous times.

The night before my first trip through the icefall, I had so many things running through my mind that yet again it made me think about life. About everything, anything, all at once. It's very hard to do something like Everest—voluntarily putting yourself in danger. I put over a year into the trip, and I was happy I had made it that far. It had truly been a test of spirit and persistence and self-exploration.

I've been to the point where I knew I was going to die. One thing I was worried about was leaving my loved ones. I wasn't sure I could do that to them. That was the biggest thought in the back of my mind—others. I wondered about the future a lot, too. It was hard being in a place like that where people *do* die, for whatever reasons, and other people don't make it.

What of me? Was I doing the right thing? Would I make it? I was told before getting into Base Camp that I was an inspiration for many because I followed my dreams and I had made it that far. Was I really doing this for inspiration, or for some selfish ideas I had? I'd say I did it for all the right reasons, because no way in hell would I actually be enjoying this: freezing my cojones off and putting my life in danger if I didn't have to. There were a lot of unknowns about this trip as well, and maybe I was having a men-tal breakdown.

Everything to come would be new to me, and I hoped it all worked out well. I hoped my body reacted well, and I hoped I could go home safely. All these questions ran though my mind constantly. I pushed them aside when I had to, but otherwise they were a constant reminder of what I had in store. Books I'd read about disasters on Everest also went through my head when I was nervous. I thought, *There has to be fun and excitement with good news.* It made me think how sadistic our society really is. We like to read about all the bad stuff more than good stuff.

Maybe that's why our society is going downhill. Maybe that's why people sue all the time and don't take responsibility for themselves. It's burned into our minds that bad things are normal. It's everywhere! Take, for instance, something that happened the day before our trek into the icefall.

A woman from another group was visited by some people from ours. Apparently, she was showing signs of HACE. I was going to give her some of our great energy bars, and someone flat-out told me, "No." We had a long chat about it, but this was what was finally concluded: If we gave her these bars and she ended up dying, the group she was with could blame us for it. If we tried to help her down and she died, again, it could be our fault.

Is there no justice in this world when people can't help others without worrying about the consequences? I mean, it's ridiculous *not* to help someone because by helping them, it gives others an excuse for their own mistakes.

All that was flying through my mind the night before leaving Base Camp to climb to the top of the Khumbu Icefall. Maybe my brain was trying to come up with other things to worry about so I wouldn't think about the skyscraper-sized hunks of ice that tumble without warning here, destroying everything in their path and killing everyone in their way.

At 4:17 A.M. I woke up to Pemba saying, "Sean . . . Sean . . ."

It was time to get out of my sleeping bag and head up this beast.

Was I ready?

Maybe; maybe not.

Either way, I was about to find out.

CHAPTER TWELVE

DAWA DORJEE

❖

I mumbled some obscenities and tried to get my warm body out of the sleeping bag and into the bone-chilling air at roughly four-thirty A.M. on Thursday, April 11. It was going to be my first trip of many through the Khumbu Icefall.

Wiggling my toes, I tried to stay warm, instead of getting cold and trying to warm up again. This high up, this bone-numbingly cold, it was always a game of trying to stay warm. Every day around three or three-thirty in the afternoon, the temperatures would go from about 70 degrees Fahrenheit to 10. That high in altitude, the sun bakes everything around, and the radiation is so intense, it makes everything scorching hot. However, when the sun goes behind a cloud or sets, the temperature plummets below zero.

Sleeping with my clothes inside the sleeping bag to keep them warm (as well as water bottles, boot liners, contact lens solution, and anything else that would freeze), I managed to get dressed inside the bag. My outfit that day consisted of long underwear, my sheep (big burly fleece), and a jacket shell. I then managed to put on my boots and meander on over to the kitchen, carefully minding my step over the boulders, large rocks, and sharp ice, where we had eggs and toast for breakfast.

Next I filled my water bottles with hot water (cold would freeze in a matter of minutes) and a pineapple powdered-drink mix, and slid them into an insulator that was basically like a gigantic beer coozie (I wish!) to keep the liquid warm. I then slipped on my harness, grabbed my ice axe, and with my trusty Sherpas, I headed out of Base Camp for our first trip up the mountain.

Many people think Everest is a single climb, nice and neat, cut and dried. I knew from research and was now living proof that the magnificent beast is anything but. You don't just start at sea level and start trekking up; along the way, there are climbs within climbs, acclimation points, training, practice, more practice, additional training, and endless, stretching climbs, each of which presents its own unique set of challenges, problems, and dangers.

Case in point: The Khumbu Icefall is one of the most dangerous sections of the entire climb. Gigantic chunks of ice the size of houses and large buildings lay scattered like a granite obstacle course. The entire glacier is moving at about four feet a day, so it's just good luck that the building-sized ice cubes don't fall and destroy everything in their path. Everywhere I looked, I saw things that could tumble down without warning. It was a matter of climbing through the right ones and weaving through the labyrinth of ice blocks (seracs) to see whether you'd succeed on any given day. Oftentimes there were gaping holes or cracks between seracs, and even crevasses where I couldn't see the bottom.

At one point I was standing at the edge of a huge block of ice and packed snow. I looked precariously over the edge and couldn't see the bottom. Off to the right, at about 45 degrees, was another crevasse that had split a glacier. Directly in front of me was a two-foot-by-two-foot chunk of ice. It was one step onto that to cross the small crevasse. It was a huge pinnacle of ice that stood alone in the middle of the crevasses with no bottom.

As I slowly stepped down onto the ice pinnacle, looking to either side into the abyss, I had my ice axe ready in case the large ice cube dropped off into nowhere. I managed to step back up about two feet onto the other side of the crevasse. I had made it safely and could continue the expedition. There was no possible way to skip the step, nor was there any other way around. All I could do was pray that the thin ice block held my weight when I jumped onto it and up to the other side. Fun stuff, and it only got better!

All through the icefall, there were flimsy aluminum ladders spanning crevasses hundreds of feet deep. It was quite nerve-racking, but I'd have to get used to crossing them. The ladders (I'm sure you're wondering) aren't there all season, and yes, they get contorted into all different shapes because of the moving seracs and the compression of the ice and glacier. They are placed there by the "icefall doctors."

This hearty group of Sherpas is paid a portion of everyone's expedition fee to go up practically every day and secure the ladders and maintain the "route" through the icefall. One ladder in particular gave me some problems at the beginning. It was four ladders tied together, spanning roughly a twenty-five-foot crevasse. I carefully placed my left foot on the rungs, immediately hearing my crampons echo through the hollow ladder and the horrible sound of metal on metal.

From there I placed my right foot in front of the left and was instantly off balance and stumbling over to my right. I jumped back as powerfully as I could and caught myself on the ice where the ladder started. Lucky for me, I had quick reactions that day, otherwise I surely would have fallen into the crevasse and hoped the guide ropes on the side of the ladder would hold my weight as I plummeted into the dark abyss that yawned, seemingly forever, below.

The problem was that my boots were a heavy size 13.5 and wide enough that they knocked into each other near the ankles. Maybe instead of trying to practice and train with all the climbing gear, learning how not to land on an ice axe, etc., I should have just practiced walking, since apparently, I couldn't even do that.

The entire time we were working our way slowly up through the shifting ice, we were in the shade of the largest mountains in the world until the sun started peeking over the 20,000-foot peaks. As we made our way up through the icefall and over countless crevasses and even more ladders, I started to develop a persistent cough that produced some very thick and disgusting brown, yellowish, green gook from the depths of my lungs.

We managed to make it just under Camp 1 (about 19,000 feet), and I couldn't stop coughing and hacking up this disgusting phlegm. Our goal had been to make it to Camp 1, but I was happy with making it nearly there. One of the Sherpas went ahead and dropped off a cache of gear, supplies, and food while I continued to cough and think about my life once again.

Naturally, I started getting nervous because I had invested so much into this trip. I was twenty-seven years old and had nothing if I didn't have this. I had no job and no place to live when we got back to Colorado. I had canceled my car insurance and never could afford real health insurance anyway, and here I was on the other side of the world, chasing a dream trying to help others by giving them hope.

What about me? What about what I needed? Here I was, ready

for the ascent, and now my body was giving out on me. Where was *my* hope? I figured I could determine that later, because if anything negative planted a seed in my brain now, it would grow into a tree of negativity I couldn't handle when I needed my sanity the most. I was on the side of Everest and determined to enjoy myself while I could. It was a once-in-a-lifetime opportunity, and I was going to make the best of it. Goal number one accomplished: having fun and making it through the Khumbu Icefall alive.

I was trying to build on each little goal I had set for myself. To accomplish the ultimate goal, I needed to set more realistic goals, so I broke the mountain down into smaller mountains, with the Khumbu Icefall being one of them. Camp 1 was another, then Camp 2, and so on up past Camp 4 and, finally, the ultimate goal: the Everest summit.

To run up Everest would be foolish and, frankly, impossible. The body needs to acclimate and get used to the thinning air, not to mention the 1,001 little things that can go wrong on the way, like, say, falling into an ice crevasse and never being heard from again. So we set for ourselves a tentative schedule of the following:

- Climb to the top of the icefall, return to Base Camp (BC).
- Rest.
- Climb to Camp 1 (C1). Sleep. Climb to Camp 2 (C2), return to BC.
- Rest.
- Climb to C2. Sleep two nights, return to BC.
- Rest.
- Climb to C2. Sleep. Climb just below Camp 3 (C3), return to C2. Sleep. Return to BC.

- Rest.
- Climb to C2. Sleep two nights, climb to C3. Sleep, return to BC.
- Rest.
- Drop lower than BC back into a village to regain my hunger and get oxygen-rich air for a few days.
- Rest.
- Hike from the lower village back to BC and wait for the weather to break and make our summit push.

So let me ask you, the reader, a question: While you're reading this, do you *really* think everything went as planned on the mountain? Knowing me, my luck, and every one of the 1,001 possible things that could go wrong up there? On the highest mountain in the world, where weather is incredibly difficult to predict and it's never what you expect to begin with? And with the way our trip had been going so far (lost passport, lost luggage, no down suit until a few days before the summit push, etc.), do you really think this is what happened? Oh, God, no! Would that we had been so lucky!

Along with that tentative schedule, I saw a doctor from another expedition and was put on antibiotics. She thought I had bronchitis. So for the first two weeks or so of climbing Everest, not only did I have to put up with my one fully functioning lung at altitude, but I also had to battle off bronchitis. Good Lord. (Or, in the words of my new hero Charlie Brown, whom I was quickly coming to resemble in the luck department, "Good grief!")

After a few nights of resting (until the weather wasn't so horrible), we were gearing up to climb to Camp 1. I would be lying if

I said I wasn't nervous the night before. I was scared, worrying about how my body would react up that high. I kept telling myself over and over again that it would be perfectly fine, that my body was going to be great, that the coughing and the phlegm and the butterflies would stop once I was suited up and had started climbing.

However, in the back of my mind, I honestly didn't know how I would be. But the reasons for the trip were always with me, and those kept me going. Meanwhile, positive thoughts kept bouncing around in my brain:

I know I'm going to make a difference in people's lives.

I hope I have a good influence on people's lives, and I also hope they see what I've done.

I want to visit hospitals and visit kids to see people and how they're doing.

I'm just some guy testing his luck and showing others what can be done.

I looked back on my life and saw a lot of setbacks and disappointments, and it seemed like one excuse after another. Now there were no excuses. It was time for that to be over. It was time for me to reflect on who I was and see that I was someone with a lot of courage. I define courage as doing something even though you're afraid of it; facing something head-on and trying your best despite the odds and the naysayers.

This is what I decided after all that soul-searching: The next day I *was* going to Camp 1, and I *was* going to enjoy every minute of it. I decided I would be like the Sherpas and not be exhausted when I got there. Maybe, I thought, I would just be a little tired of seeing white all day. I kept telling myself all that night: I am *going to do this. I am going to be successful. I am adjusting fantastically, because I know my body can handle anything I put my mind to! Tomorrow, here I come, baby!*

And tomorrow sure was surprised, if I do say so myself. I stormed up the Khumbu Icefall step for step with the Sherpas, and we got to Camp 1 with no problems at all. The entire way, my mental visualizations came true. It was almost like I was having déjà vu from the night before.

I was having a great time chatting with people on the mountain, talking to the Sherpas, even enjoying walking over the crevasses, all the while with a smile plastered on my face. It could have been the freezing cold that made it stick that way, but I'm pretty sure it was because I was enjoying the moment and having fun again. Upon arriving at Camp 1, I helped Nima Gombu cook lunch and collect snow to melt for water. We chatted about things like religion, marriage, wives, girlfriends, life—everything, to be honest. We really got to know each other up there and on the trip to Base Camp.

As a matter of fact, during the entire hike to the 17,600-foot Base Camp, we got to know each other well enough to start joking around. I was pulled into their culture. Seth and I tried the local food, not the typical tourist food the Sherpas gave to trekkers and climbers. Nima and Kame were short in stature, with dark skin, I'm guessing from the intense sun, because it was also like leather. They had black hair, very dark, squinty eyes, and were always smiling. Very quiet but powerful people. I was honored to be with the best climbers in the world, as well as one of the nicest, most caring cultures I had ever seen.

After sleeping at Camp 1 and waking up every hour on the hour, peeing four times that night, and having some crazy-freaky dreams (don't ask), I packed up, and we headed toward Camp 2, across the Western Cwm (pronounced "coom").

The Western Cwm was approximately a five-mile hike that ascended gradually uphill for an elevation gain of about 2,000 feet all told. On our hike through the Cwm, we managed to jump over countless small crevasses, hop on and over a number of other aluminum ladders, and climb into and out of a few gigantic cracks in the ice.

When we finally made it to Camp 2, I could tell my body and brain were starved for oxygen. I felt, well, weird. Not exactly scientific, but that's about the best way I can explain it. Like something just wasn't right, and I was a little off kilter. Upon arriving at Camp 2, we took some photos, hugged one another, and headed back down all the way to Base Camp, bypassing Camp 1. For the rest of the expedition, Camp 1 would be used as an emergency camp, storage, and a rest stop between Base Camp and Camp 2.

After resting a few days at Base Camp (rest days consisted of eating as much as possible—or as much as you could keep down—reading, and visiting other groups at Base Camp), we were going to head back up to Camp 2 for a couple of nights, but instead, I found myself thinking about why I was climbing and if it was really worth it after all.

I was nervous about everything, over and above the nerve-racking climb itself. This was because earlier that same day, on our way up to Camp 2, the sun was coming out and I reached to put on my glacier glasses to prevent snow blindness (burning of the cornea), but to no avail. No sunglasses. An amateur mistake, for sure, and yet another uncertain aspect of my bittersweet climb. Was I really ready? Would any of these other climbers make such a bush-league mistake? Maybe I was just tired and not thinking.

While I struggled with my on-again, off-again self-confidence, Kame and Nima Gombu kept going to take their loads to Camp 2 while I turned around in the icefall to make my way back to Base Camp. Climbing down by myself in the cold air, I could feel the glacier settling and the sound of skyscraper-sized ice cubes rubbing against one another and cracking in the warming air. Near a crevasse that I could tell was shifting, I suddenly heard a thunderous crack.

Abruptly, I was standing on top of a gigantic block of ice that settled about five feet and dropped me to my knees while pushing all the air it displaced up through the fissures and directly into the back of my head. It was like a kettle on a stove erupting with boiling water inside, but this was cold and being forced through a fissure roughly the size of a football field, gaining momentum and kick-ass force on its way through the chute.

The rest of the way down to BC, embarrassed, humiliated, humbled, and, frankly, scared to death, I was kicking stones, throwing things, and showing a sick display of attitude. After managing to get back down to Base Camp, I ate like a pig and tried to rehydrate all day, licking my wounds and regaining my composure from the day's tantrum.

After a couple of days' rest at Base Camp, we were ready to push up to Camp 2 to spend a couple of nights at 21,000 feet. Climbing through the icefall (again), over the ladders, up the ladders, and to the top of the icefall, I kept up with the group of Sherpas. When we got to the precipice on top of the icefall, we all sat down and took a little rest.

Words like "strong climber" and "very strong" kept coming

out of the Sherpas' mouths. They were telling me I was strong for keeping up with them and continuing my push up the mountain. Because I was born on a Monday, they called me Dawa (Sherpas are named after the days of the week on which they're born and are differentiated by their middle names) Dorjee (meaning strength, power, and luck). Roughly translated, I suppose, I was "Monday Powerful."

So, from then on, Dawa Dorjee was my name. We made it the rest of the way to Camp 2 in a "Sherpa group," calling one another by the days of the week and scrambling upward through adversity to find purchase on our dreams. (Or, at least, *my* dream.)

I often wondered during that phase of the climb if it was the alternating altitudes that made my mood swings so prominent, or the reality of what I was doing setting in. Being newly christened by the Sherpas was a major achievement. I recalled the first time we met and how they'd ransacked my rucksack to find it unacceptable. I realized, too, that it had taken me a few weeks to prove to them that I could handle the undertaking. Their confidence gave me a new sense of purpose and another reason to keep a handle on my emotions. (After all, I didn't want to be labeled Monday Tantrum!)

Upon making our way to Camp 2, we organized the rest of the camp with rock walls between our tents, facing each other to keep out the wind and horrible weather. That night I had the most horrible dream ever. Without going into detail, I was in a coffin and couldn't move. I was trapped underground, buried—dead.

Maybe it was because I hadn't eaten properly in about five days and was malnourished by that point of the trek. Maybe it was because I was climbing with two people who didn't speak

English very well. It was incredibly lonely on the mountain at times, and difficult to explain certain things to the Sherpas. Things like "I don't have an appetite" would come across, roughly translated, as if I merely had indigestion. They'd ask if I had medicine for it, and when I told them no, they couldn't understand why. It wasn't my stomach, and I couldn't explain that to them. Sleeping in the tent alone without a climbing partner to chat with, all my thoughts to myself, my nervousness, my pain, all kept inside and festered. I had my brother at Base Camp, but our radios didn't work past Camp 1 because we didn't have a large antenna, only handheld two-way radios.

At Base Camp, Seth kept me company. We played cards, read books, talked about Mom and Dad, our girlfriends at the time, what we were going to do when we got back home, and what we were going to eat first the minute we were back in "civilization," i.e., within fifty miles of the nearest fast food joint. Funny thing is, when you're out in the middle of one of the most inhospitable places in the world, eating strange food, you crave the strangest things, like steak and ice cream.

Whenever I came back from the mountain and stumbled into Base Camp, Seth was always there, taking care of me with water, helping me out of my boots, and listening to me describing the route higher up. It must have been difficult for him to be there alone when I was climbing, but he befriended a number of people around Base Camp to help pass the time.

Before we left the States, we had come to terms with the fact that he wouldn't be able to climb, and we were going to do everything possible to get me and everyone touched by cancer to the summit. Saying goodbye early in the morning wasn't too difficult, and it was always nice to come back to family, especially because Seth spoke English.

On the mountain, I was essentially alone. I had my journal and my thoughts to keep me company. I tried to learn as much as I could from the Sherpas and did what they did while on the side of Everest, but that only lasted so long. Whenever I got the opportunity to talk to other climbers, I did so quite enthusiastically (as you might imagine) and, in the process, met people from Dubai, Russia, Switzerland, England, and all over the world. In that respect, I was lucky, and that was what I focused on.

After being "stuck" in Camp 2 for a while, and with the weather not letting up for our trip to Camp 3, we decided to return to Base Camp to refuel our bodies with more food and relax at the much lower altitude. Hiking through the Cwm toward Camp 1, however, we couldn't see a thing. It was a complete whiteout with tremendous winds; it was, quite literally, snowing sideways. This became my first official experience with an infamous Everest storm. I was taken aback when we made it through Camp 1 and into the Khumbu Icefall again. Just 2,000 feet lower, and it felt like an oven. From fearing the sideways snow a little while earlier, now I thought I would pass out from dehydration. The extremes were intense and had effects that went far beyond the external. My body was starving for food, and I was running on empty; however, I was imagining how good I would feel when my tank was full.

Back in Base Camp, we no longer ate in separate tents, forgoing the setup of a mess tent for the clients (my brother and me) and a kitchen for the Sherpas (Kame, Nima Gombu, and Pemba). On a normal Everest expedition, there can be as many as thirty people climbing the mountain, so they make that distinction. I believe we were lucky in that we managed to get to know our friends on a personal level. In fact, there was another group south of us ordering their Sherpas around like servants.

"What the fuck do you think you're doing?" we could hear them screaming—talk about a tantrum—when the wind was blowing the right way. "I don't pay you to sit here and play cards! I pay you to haul my shit and fix the rope. I don't pay you to drink and lay around. As long as I'm here, I'm in charge, and what I say goes! Until the expedition is over, get off your asses and get my shit done!"

Wow. I couldn't believe it, because later that night, we were all having dinner in the kitchen, playing cards, drinking chang, and having a good time. (Chang is a local alcoholic beverage with a very peculiar tangy taste—the fermenting process is sped up by the women who make it, sitting around a big kettle, stirring and spitting into the mixture! Yummy.)

In contrast I made friends with the Sherpas on the mountain, and we tried to help one another along the way. Because Nima and Kame were great guys, a lot of the other Sherpas were hanging around our campsite, and we all joked around. I think Seth and I were one of the luckiest groups on the mountain, because if something did happen to me, my life would have been saved before anyone else's, and by the best climbers in the world.

We rested at Base Camp that day and then moved to Camp 2 for a couple of nights. I began thinking about what I was doing again. If I became the first cancer survivor to summit Everest, how would the story get out? I had no idea what I could do to get the news out so other people could have confidence to chase their dreams and make their own tremendous goals a reality, as I'd tried so hard to do. I prayed every night that my dreams would come true and I would make it to the top to inspire other cancer patients and survivors.

The reason for this entire expedition was to provide some sort of hope and inspiration. To encourage people to believe in themselves, to follow their own dreams, and to go after their own goals, whatever they may be. To help people live life and not sit by and watch it play out before them. I was hoping to encourage people to become active members of life. It's almost like a gym membership, and people should make the most out of it instead of letting their membership expire without first trying out the equipment. Don't just sit there making excuses as to why you aren't participating, because one day the membership will expire.

After we'd rested at Base Camp and slept like babies, it was time for us to make our last push before the last push. That's right, we were heading up to Camp 3, at nearly 24,000 feet, and sleeping on the side of the Lhotse Face. The Lhotse Face is a huge ice shelf about one mile long, at a 45-degree angle, if not steeper. Tents are placed here by chipping into the ice and snow and carving out enough of the frosty stuff to make a somewhat level ground. One tiny fraction of a mistake, and I could go rocketing down over a mile into a crevasse, killing myself in the process.

Every step felt like it was my last as the thin air bit into my lungs, forcing me to take a few minutes' rest before crawling another step forward. I sure didn't feel like Monday Powerful, that was for sure! Slowly, we crawled up the side of the ice face and into our tent. Eating dinner and trying to fall asleep were nearly impossible. The next morning I woke up, threw up, and looked to see what I'd had the night before for nourishment: carrots, peas, noodles . . . Nothing was even remotely digested. It was disgusting, because after climbing back into Base Camp, my stomach was full of gastric juices, and I had severe heartburn.

Camp 3 wasn't exactly like the Four Seasons; however, the view was breathtaking. Because our tent was chipped into and stationed on the side of the ice face, I could lean my head out and see nothing but sky and peaks of other mountains. Clouds rolled in once in a while and covered up where Camp 2 was, but behind me and up the intense slope was one of the highest mountains in the world—Lhotse. Off to my left was Nuptse, and on my right, where the route was going, I could see the South Summit of Everest and its infamous spindrift coming off the top. Even though the view was incredible, the sights magnificent, I didn't get a wink of sleep and felt like the night would never end. I managed to throw up in the Western Cwm and the icefall as well. Seth said he saw me coming down in the icefall, and it looked like I did one of those heave-hos. My head back, my back arched, I tossed everything forward in a whipping motion, releasing whatever was left in my stomach onto the ice. Maybe a rest at Base Camp would do my body good before heading down to Debuche and into lower altitudes to regain my strength, breathe oxygen-rich air, and refuel with constant food.

April 30 was the day Everest took her first life of that climbing season. On the trek into Base Camp, I had befriended a fellow from England. We'd chatted, gotten to know each other, and become instant friends. Later, we saw each other on the mountain a number of times. It was this same fellow—Peter—who managed to tumble over and over down the Lhotse Face nearly 3,000 feet into a crevasse. That very day I had talked with him while I was coming down the face, hugged him hello, chatted for a while, hugged him goodbye, and wished him all the best of luck and said we'd meet up again in Base Camp.

Those were the last words I ever said to him.

When I heard the news, my heart sank and my stomach dropped. I thought about his parents and how they were going to feel when they heard the news. And then I started thinking about my own life and who decides what happens. Who could have known he was to take one wrong step and then, in an instant, rocket down to his death? And who was the one to decide his fate?

When I was on the Lhotse Face, I imagined what it would be like to fall, and maybe that kept me extra careful. Maybe that's why I didn't fall. Then again, who knows? Maybe Peter had felt just like me—cautious, careful, wary—and fallen anyway. Maybe one gust of wind or one step in either direction were all that separated me from Peter. It put things into perspective again and made me wonder if the mountain was worth my life. No. My body and soul are worth more than a hunk of rock and ice. Period.

I called Mom and Dad to let them know it wasn't me in the papers when they read the headlines ANONYMOUS CLIMBER DIES ON EVEREST. (Nice of the newspapers to worry every single family who had a climber on the mountain, huh?) Both of them started crying, as did I.

Life tosses people curveballs once in a while to see how they handle them. I've thought about my future and what I want to do, but what if I don't ever get to any of that? Granted, positive thinking and being active and persistent have a lot to do with success and being happy, but what if fate or God or whatever you believe in has something else in store for you?

What if you have one set of plans and they don't parallel what's going to happen in your life? What's *supposed* to happen? I guess the only way to find out is by doing something. Trial and error are life; life is trial and error. Learning from mistakes is key. In fact, those mistakes aren't mistakes at all. They're different opportunities for us to learn something from what we've done. It is also those mistakes that make us unique individuals, and it's up to us to take advantage of the opportunities to make the best out of situations.

Peter dying that day proves this point. He was doing what he loved. You never know when your time is up, so try to enjoy every moment of living. I don't want to be ninety years old, wishing I had done something with my life, or wishing I'd tried something different. I don't want any "what if" questions.

So with that in mind, I was ready to move down in altitude from Base Camp, to get some food in my system and get ready for the summit push up the mountain so I wouldn't have that "what if" question of climbing Everest nipping at my heels for the rest of my life.

I had done the training. My mind was ready. True, I'd had a few setbacks, and (like any brothers) things weren't always copacetic between my brother and me during training, but he was there supporting me just the same. That's what families are supposed to do for each other; that's what brothers are bound to do for each other.

Sure, we had our little skirmishes and typical sibling arguments back in Colorado, but what was done was done, and we both knew this was my time to see what my body could do; to test if I was worthy of climbing the highest mountain in the world. It was my opportunity to provide hope to people lying in hospital beds and to do what I could to inspire people around the world to chase after their own dreams and shoot for the stars.

It would soon be time to put my body to a challenge and head back up Everest one last time.

CHAPTER THIRTEEN

THE CURVED HORIZON

❖

May 11, 2002, dawned early and bright. I'd slept fitfully the previous night, kind of like a little kid on Christmas Eve, but the sleep was good nonetheless. After preparations and good wishes, the inevitable layering of protective gear and some food in our bellies, we were finally getting ready to leave Base Camp one last time and get on our way up Everest. After the acclimatization period, my body was ready for the altitude, and my mind was ready for the summit push.

By now I had heard it all from everyone who was excited for me to make it, from "good luck" to "break a leg" to "no sleeping above Camp 4" (sleeping above C4 means you'll die, because you'll freeze to death).

A small group of fellow climbers, my brother, and well-wishers followed Kame and me to the edge of the icefall. We hugged them, headed up the long, initial ice pillar, and waved goodbye from our lofty perch. It was the last direct visual contact they would have of us until we got back down into Base Camp. They could see us from camp through binoculars and really good zoom cameras, and we could have radio communication the entire time, but it wouldn't replace the physical one-on-one we shared that fateful morning.

Without much fanfare, I donned my bright yellow gator boots and trucked up the mountain. Kame and I were like supermen going up the Khumbu Icefall. We kept passing people with ease. With determination in my heart, a pack on my back, and my feet feeling light as feathers, I was up and through the icefall in no time. The ladder crossings over the crevasses didn't faze me, and the last long ice climb up to the edge of the Khumbu was no problem. Nothing was getting in my way. I felt like a horse with blinders on, my steps steady and sure, my mind focused and free. I had one goal in mind, and nothing was going to distract me. Nothing.

When I set a goal for myself and I'm intent on making it, I focus on that goal and let nothing get in my way of accomplishing it. This was no different. Granted, I did have doubts, just like anyone would, but I knew I was here for a reason, and I was excited to see where I could go and how high. I had decided that no matter what happened above Camp 4, the expedition was already a success, and the summit would be a bonus. Getting to the top was the icing on the cake. I was out to have fun, to enjoy the trip, but in the back of my mind, I knew I was going to make it.

Normally, it takes about eight to nine hours to get to Camp 2. A mere five hours later, we were sitting in our tents, relaxing with some water and fruit juice, nibbling on dried food. I hung with the Sherpas all the way up to 21,000 feet, then dropped my pack in the tent and turned around to help some others get their stuff up to Camp 2. I got there full of energy and ready to go, but unfortunately, I wouldn't be able to keep up the momentum, although this time it was through no fault of my own. We were going to stay at Camp 2 for two nights to recover from the trip and let the weather get a little better.

Rumor had it from the Sherpa grapevine that the weather would be good on the fifteenth, so we adjusted our schedule once again. The infamous Sherpa grapevine was as reliable as it was mysterious. No one knew the weather patterns, but the Sherpas somehow got things they needed, be it information, grapes, fresh veggies, or even a battery.

Believe it or not, that's exactly what happened to Seth. He needed a battery, asked Pemba for one, and a couple of days later, like magic, there it was. It was empty, so he asked again, this time for the acid to pour into the cells and give it juice. I'm sure you can imagine what happened a couple of days later. Just like magic . . . acid! To top it all off, my summit suit arrived in a brown box labeled SEAN SWARNER; EVEREST BASE CAMP. I have no idea how it got there, given the lack of facilities or even ways to identify a snowsuit-clad climber, but it arrived a few days before the summit push. Like I said, pure magic.

Camp 2 was our resting place for a couple of days before we headed back up the Lhotse Face again. The same face I had climbed down to hug Peter hello and goodbye and wish him good luck. The same face he had tumbled down to his death. The same 45-degree-angled parking lot that dumped unwary or unprepared or just plain unlucky climbers into a vast and endless crevasse. As unfortunate as it was, if I was going to make the summit of Everest, I had to go back up the same route that had taken the life of my friend.

After a couple of days sleeping at 21,000 feet, Nima joined our group, Kame headed up in front of us to Camp 4, and we made our way up the mile-long sheet of ice. That day was deceptively beautiful. A picture-postcard day to cloak the setting of many a climber's own personal horror flick. Warm weather, the sun was high, no clouds, and most important, no wind. Earlier that night we could hear the jet stream pummeling over the summit of Everest, howling at well over two hundred miles an hour. We were heading up there soon, and I hoped the weather was going to cooperate.

On the thirteenth of May, we were resting at Camp 3, trying to rehydrate and get some food inside us. Instant mashed potatoes had been the only thing that was appetizing to me the last time I was up there, but this time was different. I had chocolate, tons of water, and as many noodles as I could shove into my belly. I was hungry, and that's not normal. Most people at this altitude have no hunger and no real thirst, either. It's usually difficult to keep much down, if anything gets swallowed to begin with.

Not me. I was feeling incredible and having such a fantastic time. Going up the Lhotse Face, we caught people and managed to talk the entire way up. Now, don't get me wrong, we weren't exactly running up the ice face, but we *were* enjoying our trip.

Passing people going slower than us, not apologizing for our pace, we boogied to our tent like Boy Scouts on parade. Our plan was to sleep there and head to Camp 4 the next day, rest, and head up for the summit that night to summit the next morning. No problem; no biggie. Everything was going incredibly well—in fact, even better than we'd expected. All was completely fine that night. I slept like a baby until early in the morning, when I couldn't sleep anymore. We were doing perfectly fine until I woke up. Something had happened. Something horrible had happened to me with no explanation, no warning, no nothing.

The something was . . . I couldn't walk.

My feet would simply not go one in front of the other anymore. Slight problem when you're hanging out at 24,000 feet on the side of an ice field at a 45-degree angle. For whatever reason, my brain was thinking clearly, I just couldn't walk. I couldn't stumble, punt, or run, and I certainly couldn't climb.

Hell, I could barely dress myself. Putting my boots on took about thirty minutes or more. Before I left Base Camp, I had told Seth that he was officially my eyes and ears while I was in altitude. I knew a lot of times people got up there and their brain wouldn't function well enough to think. Sometimes it's like your body is severely intoxicated and you think your mind is perfectly fine, but no matter what you do or how hard you concentrate, it's impossible to get your body to do what you want it to. On the other hand, you could think you're okay, though your body is doing crazy things, and it's impossible to know you're out of your element and killing yourself.

So before I left Base Camp, I told Seth he was going to make the decisions for me if something came up, and I was going to listen to him no matter what. He got in touch with another group on the mountain, a rather large group with a very large budget, and they were nice enough to let Seth communicate with me via their radio. I ended up using their frequency from then on, and if I needed Seth, they would go get him and have him chat with me. Either that or they'd radio to him on another channel and relay messages to him on my behalf. It was like that every time I'd head up the mountain, and we were lucky to befriend them.

This experience—this not walking—was different. It was the first time my life was in danger, and we didn't know what to do about it. Seth was on the other line, and we tried to determine the next plan of action.

There are two altitude-related problems that can happen on the side of a large mountain and endanger your life. There are more, enough to fill a college textbook, but in this case there were only two we were really concerned about. One is HAPE, or high-altitude pulmonary edema. HAPE occurs when fluid collects in the lungs from the atmospheric pressure and altitude change. It causes a gurgling in the lungs every time air flows in and out. What eventually happens is the person with HAPE drowns on the fluid in his or her lungs and dies. This wasn't happening to me. I wasn't coughing, nor did I have any fluid in my lungs.

The other, more severe problem is HACE, or high-altitude cerebral edema. This is altitude-induced swelling of the brain, brought upon by the same things as HAPE but much more serious. When this happens, the person loses consciousness and dies. The cure for both of these altitude-related conditions is an immediate decrease in altitude, to bring the body back into a homeostatic state again, one where the body is regulated and in balance.

To check for HACE, one popular indicator is the infamous walk-a-line test, just like a field sobriety test, where the subject walks a line, heel, toe, heel, toe. I was going to do the same thing. Needless to say, it was nearly impossible to find a three-foot flat area in Camp 3, but, like kids on a snow-covered playground, the Sherpas stomped down and flattened out a small area for me to try. I was to climb out of the tent, radio back to Seth, and let him know the results of this test.

After the thirty minutes of fumbling around with my boots, I managed to get outside and try the test. After repeated failure of one foot randomly landing to either side of my planted foot, I knew something was deadly wrong. As I radioed back to Seth with tears in my eyes, I thought the expedition was over. I thought my body had hit its limit and I could go no higher.

I thought it had all been for naught, that I had done all this—gotten the funding, cashed in my entire life savings, trained on baked potatoes and ramen noodles in Colorado, flown halfway around the world, dragged along my little brother and the hopes and dreams of countless people touched by cancer—all to see the mountaintop but never reach it.

Seth and I then decided the expedition was already a success. We gave ourselves a big, fat pep talk to see us through the night. We would rest at Camp 3 for the day and sleep on oxygen that night. On the fifteenth, I would see how I was feeling and make a decision then. It was kind of like putting my hope on layaway; come the fifteenth, I'd see whether or not I could afford it.

As great as this plan sounded, every other group at Camp 3 with us that day headed up to Camp 4 while we rested. They were going to attempt a summit on the fifteenth, our initial projected summit date. One of the friends I had made on the trip was heading up, and though we'd had plans of being on the summit together, this just wasn't in the cards.

But waking up the next day after an amazing night's sleep, I felt like Superman again. I was back to my old self, joking around, smiling, and enjoying everything. It was like night and day. I didn't know what had happened that night during my sleep, but I didn't care. I'd had enough self-examination; now it was time to take life at face value, to appreciate what came my way, and not to ask too many questions to make it happen all over again.

Everest, it would seem, has her own perverse sense of justice. Inexperienced climbers prevail where climbing legends fail, weather comes and weather goes, hopes are dashed and dreams are made, and the best-laid plans are often those that wind up turning dreams into drama. For me, Everest had been a harsh but fair mistress. Whether I deserved a second chance or not remained to be seen, but because of the way things had played out, I would get to find out.

Others weren't so lucky. As it turned out, no one who left on the fifteenth made the summit. They ran into bad weather and had to turn back for Camp 4, losing their window of opportunity to climb. Each climber can carry only so many bottles of oxygen, so they get one summit attempt each year. If they don't make it, there's no turning back and trying for a second attempt.

If I hadn't been sick, if I hadn't needed to sit that day out and recuperate, I would have been in the same summit party with every other unsuccessful attempt on the fifteenth. I came down with what we thought was minor cerebral edema, making it impossible for me to climb to Camp 4, therefore making me absent from the group heading for the top on the day we were supposed to. Lucky? Oh, good Lord, you bet. I think I have the world's worst good luck (so many bad things happen to me, but somehow I come out okay in the end) and, on top of that, a group of guardian angels working on overtime, turning lemons into lemonade (when they aren't too busy turning water into wine!). I just pray to God they never go on vacation, because I'll be in some serious trouble.

Climbing out of Camp 3 through a rather long traverse, we caught some people before the Yellow Band. The Yellow Band is rightfully named because of a thick yellowish band of rock flowing down with the slope of the mountain between visible layers of gray and black rock. There was no snow but a gigantic ridge of rock sandwiching this peculiar yellow band. People were going so slowly up this rock face that we passed people on our way.

Keep in mind that if we took one small step in the wrong direction, or lost our footing, Nima and I would have rocketed down, tumbling over two miles to our death. Not a pleasant thought at all. Not one bit. We were very careful, but also so intent on making it to Camp 4 and the infamous Death Zone that we wouldn't let anything get in our way. Not yellow rock, black rock, gray rock, or rock of any height, angle, or color. We moved over for some Sherpas coming down from the high camp, and were courteous to the other climbers, but we kept moving as quickly as we could, essentially storming up the mountain.

After reaching the top of the Yellow Band, we took a break and had some water and food. I was listening to my MP3 player, jamming out to some tunes and enjoying the incredible day, as if perhaps I were Rollerblading in Central Park or hanging from a 14er in Colorado. We had radio contact with Base Camp through the larger antenna, so Seth knew where we were the entire time and how close we were getting to the last camp. The tension was clear in our voices, but so was the triumph. We didn't need words to reflect on how far we'd come, how many times we could have been turned back—by illness, fate, lost luggage or passports— and how much we'd already accomplished by making it this far. Still, the icing on the cake was slowly, so slowly, getting closer.

The final obstacle before the high camp was the Geneva Spur, an outcropping of rock jutting from the side of Everest. It was almost as if a small mountain had pierced Everest's crust and given her a tumor, and climbers for generations a giant pain in the arse.

This tumor that we had to climb up and over had countless ropes hanging from it, left by years of previous expeditions. Which one was I to grab and use as a guide? I had no idea; every rope on Everest has a history, and most of them are mysteries. I roped into a number of them and prayed they would hold my weight if I lost my footing. I couldn't worry about that now and focused on the goal at hand—getting to 26,000 feet and the final

---

camp. A couple of tumors had tried to get the best of me in my teens. No way was *this* tumor getting the best of me.

My crampons bit into the rock, wedged themselves between frozen rocks and ice. It was slow and precarious going, like trying to walk to school by only touching the cracks in the sidewalk, double-stepping sometimes and stretching beyond one's limits at others. Slowly making my way up this massive rock outcropping, I prayed I wouldn't slip and die. Death was around every corner, but I couldn't focus on it.

As with battling cancer, climbing Everest was an uphill struggle, and I did my best not to let my mind drift from the task. If I did, I wouldn't be alive. Period. I knew I was going to make it, I knew everything was going to be okay. That was the attitude to take, the only attitude worth having, the only attitude one could have. Topping out on the Geneva Spur, we had a short (when I say short, I mean a couple of hours—it's all in proportion to the size of Everest) hike to the South Col, where we would find Camp 4 at last.

As we rounded the corner on the side of the Geneva Spur, the South Col and Camp 4 spread out before me, with Everest directly in front of me. Stretching for what seemed like miles was a gradual uphill slope leading toward the summit ridge and the last 3,000 feet of the climb. To my right was the summit ridge of Lhotse, rocks plastered with snow and wind-swept. I had made it into the Death Zone. Above 26,000 feet (only fourteen mountains in the world are this high), the body starts to deteriorate with each step. Muscle breaks down, fat melts away, and the mind starts to go. It's called the Death Zone not because so many people have died here but because the body literally starts to decompose. The more time spent at this altitude, the more the body dies.

Radioing down to Seth and the others following my progress at Base Camp, I jokingly said to my brother, "Dude, you should see this thing. It's huge!" Duh, it's Everest, the largest mountain in the world. What did I think it was going to be like?

Our plan was to get into Camp 4, try to eat, and rest until about nine P.M. Then we would get up, get dressed, and head up the mountain for the twelve-hour push to the summit. The entire time, we were "sleeping" (no real sleeping happens here because of the altitude) with our oxygen masks on; however, every once in a while I'd take it off, walk around, and see how it was without the extra O's. I did a great job and was feeling incredibly well.

After dining by the romantic light of headlamps and downing a few bowls of instant mashed potatoes (I actually had an appetite up that high, which is very rare) and a couple of chocolate bars, Kame, Nima Gombu, and I lay down to rest and try to sleep. Wearing my down suit and sleeping in my minus-40-degree bag, I stayed warm. I also had my boots, my liners, my extra socks, and everything inside the bag with me to keep it warm. One of the worst feelings is sliding warm feet into cold boots that high up. It sucks the warmth right from your feet, and there is no getting the warmth back once that happens; they're cold for the entire day, and you get frostbite and lose toes.

I woke up to Nima shaking me and saying, "Sean, Sean. Get up!" I sat upright from a deep sleep, not really knowing what was going on, but I pulled myself together and started getting dressed. It was ten P.M., one hour after we were supposed to be *leaving* the South Col. We were late and not just off protocol but off target; we were jeopardizing our turnaround time.

Every expedition has a set time to turn around, and no matter how close the group is to the summit (twenty feet, ten feet, five feet, whatever), they turn around. Period. End of story. It's simply too dangerous to continue and risk running into bad weather and not making it down safely. Businesspeople and top negotiators have a walkaway point, the point at which a deal is too rich for their blood or not good enough to pursue, when they get up and leave the table, no matter how close they are to a deal. The turnaround is a climber's ultimate walkaway point. Remember the suggestion of not sleeping above Camp 4 because you'd die? Well, having a turnaround time is one thing you can do to try to prevent sleeping above 26,000 feet.

Weather comes in on Everest in a heartbeat. One minute it will be sunny and warm, the next it will be minus-30, cloudy with hurricane-force winds. It's like living in the middle of a science experiment at the top of the world: no warning, no mercy. We were putting not just our climb but our lives in danger by leaving so late and so far behind everyone else attempting a summit that same night/day.

After getting everything on, we started out for the summit push. As I looked up at the enormous mountain in front of me (because of the headlamps of the countless other climbers, I could see the outline, and the moon helped as well), a smile came over my face and any nervousness left my mind. I radioed down to Seth at Base Camp and said, "Well, we're the last to leave Camp Four. We better get going."

And that's what we did. Moving quickly across the rather flat area to where the true heart of the mountain started, we trudged uphill at a nearly 40-degree angle. We attached ourselves to the fixed lines and put on our jumars as well. Jumars slide up rope but not down, and they help in climbing. I used them carefully and often. Damn if I was going to slip and fall to my death after coming this far, this fast.

We slugged ourselves up the mountain through the four-foot-deep snow. This high in altitude, with your body wasting away at every footstep, if a climber is averaging five feet in a minute, he's making good time. A step and a rest. A step and a rest. Breathing about twenty times between steps, most people don't climb up the mountain, they inch up.

Nima Gombu, Kame, and I caught the group going up and were going about thirty or so steps before resting to breathe. It was incredible how I felt on the side of the mountain. I had no doubt in my mind that I was going to make it. Parts of my body might have been dying with each footfall, but my brain was alive and well.

The first place to rest was a relatively flat area called the Balcony. We managed to get to the Balcony before more than half the group. We unclipped from the guide ropes and made our own route to the ridge. We were in our own world, our own zone within the Death Zone, passing people left and right. Even looking to my left and seeing a mangled mess of a body didn't faze me. That's right: I passed a dead body on the mountain. On the same mountain I was trying to climb and summit. The same mountain he died on and I might have as well but didn't.

After hitting the Balcony while the others rested, we kept climbing. Here most people changed oxygen bottles, but we were still going strong. We had three bottles for each person, and we had set the flow rate lower than necessary, so we hadn't run out yet. On the oxygen bottles, there's a regulator, and you can set the flow rate to so many liters per minute. It's not like scuba diving, where every time you breathe in, air flows into the lungs, and every time you breathe out, a valve closes and oxygen stops.

We kept going and caught the top climbers, who were leading the group to the summit. Partway to the South Summit, my feet started getting cold and went numb. On the ridge, I bounced in my boots to keep blood flowing to my toes. Next step, I'd bounce some on the other toes. I wasn't sure what was happening, and there was no way I could check, because it was bone-chilling cold and I was wearing two pairs of gloves and a pair of huge over-mitts. If I took my hands out, they'd instantly freeze. My face was covered by a balaclava and hat as well as the oxygen mask. Goggles covered the rest of my face, so not a single bit of skin was exposed.

After we caught the climbers, we stayed behind them and slowed down quite a bit. It was a good thing, because just then hundred-mile-an-hour winds came shooting over the ridge and tried to knock us off the side of the mountain, like a convoy of eighteen-wheelers swooping down on us.

Jabbing my ice axe into the snow, using it as an anchor, I stabilized myself to not get blown off the side of the mountain. After a number of gigantic gusts that nearly took our lives, it was dead calm. No wind. No memory of wind. Nothing. In fact, to my right, the sun started coming up.

Just another day in paradise.

Before my eyes rose a sea of beautiful reds, blues, purples, oranges, yellows, and the cusp of the sun rounding over the tops of mountains in the distance in a sea of clouds. It was free and clear of haze and pollution, like a picture in a frame scrubbed free after being buried under years of dust and mold. It was the sky as Mother Nature intended it, unsullied by humans.

Mountaintops and peaks poking through the clouds looked like islands in a sea of white with the sun as the backdrop. The most beautiful sunrise I had ever seen in my life was coming up over the horizon, and it was so close, so clean and clear, I felt like I could reach out and touch it. The horizon, I noticed, was not flat. It wasn't like I was on the ocean, at sea level, or even in the Rocky Mountains, where the sunrise and horizon were flat. I was up so high, with nothing hindering my view of the sunrise. Best of all, I could see that the earth was curved. The horizon was curved, and it was the most beautiful thing I had ever seen in my life. Until I looked to my left and saw the black sky. Poking through the night sky were stars. I was so high, I didn't *have* to look up. Directly out at eye level were stars, a sea of stars floating in the inky blackness of pure, pristine night. To my right was the most amazing sunrise, to my left a dazzling array of undiluted stars. It seemed a fitting reward for a climb well done.

At the South Summit, we took a break. The sun was up, people were catching us and collecting on the South Summit, queuing up as the day began. It was a rounded top of snow, a couple of bumps, actually, like natural picnic benches at the top of the world, and people sat down to rest. From here the route led a little down (yes, down), a traverse on the side of a snow slope to the Hillary Step, then a long snow-walk to the summit of the world.

I made my way down from the South Summit, carefully placing my feet and minding my steps (one wrong step and I'd plummet down about a mile and a half to my death and straight into Camp 2, just another statistic for the Everest logbooks). I was hoping my crampons would hold my body on the snow, ice, and rock, since all sense of gravity or logic seemed to be missing here.

The day was still spectacular, with no clouds in the sky and nature's fireworks flaring on either side of me. At the Hillary Step, there was a large V cut out of the snow drift. The drift was formed from wind sweeping up the mountain and being projected off the rock like a shark fin. A step too high on this would make the fin snap off, and this time I wouldn't land in Camp 2; I'd fall a couple of miles down into Tibet.

Just below the Hillary Step that V-shaped window into Tibet had incredible views. Again, the earth's horizon was curved. I couldn't stop smiling, my own lips curving to match the rounded perspective (but upside down, of course). We had to wait our turn behind a few climbers going up the Hillary Step. I couldn't believe it: another unexpected moment on a trip full of the unexpected. I felt like a kid waiting to ride Space Mountain at Disney World, lined up behind sunburned tourists, each fiddling with a fanny pack or Nikon while I rocked, impatient and grumpy, back and forth on the balls of my feet.

Only one person could climb through at a time, and the other climbers were going incredibly slowly. Taking a step and resting for what seemed like five minutes or more, then another step before a five-minute pit stop, there, with the summit in reach and a life's dream for the taking. A couple of climbers did this, and while they did, I turned around to see the circus of people coming up behind us: all the people we'd passed on the way up, and I was so glad we did, because we were in front of every single one of them.

At last. My turn on the step. There were countless ropes from earlier expeditions, and I grabbed a handful of them, praying at least one would hold me when I pulled myself up. Thankfully, they did, and I got to the top of the first step and rounded a rock that was jutting out from the side of the mountain. Hugging the rock, I edged my way around to the other part of the step and worked my way up. One hand on the right, my left foot to the left, and my right foot behind me. After working my way up the small chimney-like climb, I was on top.

I could finally see the summit. I knew I was going to make it. I knew that all Seth and I had been through was worth it, that every step, every ounce of blood, sweat, and tears had been worth it. My goal would not go uncompleted, my mission was not impossible. In fact, it was at hand.

Tears welled up in my eyes and started to drip down, fogging up my goggles. I removed them; by this time it was warmer, and I was wearing only two pairs of gloves. On this last leg of the journey, I removed my goggles and replaced them with my glacier glasses. I was climbing to the summit of the world, and I knew I was going to make it. The entire earth was stretched out below me, and I could see forever. At 9:32 A.M. (only ten and a half hours after we'd left Camp 4) on May 16, 2002, I stepped out from the shadows of Everest and onto the highest point on earth.

However, I was not alone. Every single person who has ever been touched by cancer was with me. The silk flag with names of people affected by cancer was with me. Every person who had ever had cancer, was battling cancer, or didn't win the fight with their cancer was right there with me. And for those who had passed away, I knew I was close enough to heaven to call out to them, "Hello."

I radioed down to my brother, and we both started crying, knowing what I had just done. Seth got on the phone to Mom and Dad and said, "At this moment in time, you have a son who's standing on top of the world." Still emotional after having the flag with me for so many days, I opened it up, took some pictures, and wrapped it around the top of the world, forever commemorating the struggle of cancer patients everywhere. The flag blowing in the gentle breeze, the people touched by cancer, and every single one of them was on that summit with me. I just hope you get some inspiration out of my efforts, because if a two-time cancer survivor with only one fully functioning lung can climb the highest mountain in the world, you can do anything you set your mind to.

I'm living proof of that.

ACKNOWLEDGMENTS

There are many many people I'd like to thank for supporting me through the years and for bringing me to where I am today. They've been behind me from the beginning and if weren't for these people, I probably wouldn't be alive.

First and foremost, I want to thank everyone in the world touched by cancer. Thank you for being my inspiration while climbing, training, and even while having a difficult day. I hope I can return the favor and give you some hope and inspiration to climb your own figurative Everest.

Mom and Dad . . . where do I begin? Obviously if it weren't for you, I literarily wouldn't be here, but without your constant support, encouragement, and even nagging, I wouldn't have half the motivation and drive that I possess. Seth, words alone cannot begin to describe how much I appreciate your being there for me, supporting me—not only emotionally, but monetarily as well—and helping me with your encouragement and faith in my abilities. Everest wouldn't have been possible without you. My grandma and grandpa have also been a tremendous help and support, and I hope I can make my family proud.

In the medical world, I want to thank all the oncologists, nurses, volunteers, staff, et al. in hospital systems who constantly battle this disease every day of their lives. In mine, Jennifer and Doc Davis were keys to my survival. Thanks to the Evergreens on Fall River and the Hanson family for providing lodging while training and for so selflessly supporting this cause. All my friends, including Brendan, Pat, Lupe, and Maurer, thank you for always holding me to my word and for letting me borrow books and CDs that assisted in my success. The entire town of Willard for rallying behind me and helping me through the battle against two cancers. Ben, my manager and vice president of the CancerClimber Association, for having complete faith in the Association and my dream. All my sponsors listed in the book—thank you for believing I could climb this mountain and shout from the rooftops of the world that cancer is not a death sentence, but a speed bump in life on the way to something greater. Wongchu, Kame, and Nima Gombu for not only making Everest possible, but an incredible success. Harvey, my literary agent, who has been nothing but incredible during this whole book process—thank you for helping me every step of the way. Peter and everyone at Atria, thank you for taking a gamble on my story and my life. Without your faith in me, this story would have gone untold. And last but not least—Rusty. I'm not even sure I can thank you enough because you took my jumbled words and turned them into this book.

Thank you, everyone, for helping me reach heights beyond what anyone thought possible. And again, thank you to every single person in the world touched by cancer. This is for you.